Unc
Vision

Matt Hendrick

hendrickmedia

HendrickMedia.com

HendrickMedia, LLC.
Printed in the United States of America
First printing: June 2024
ISBN# 9798325597527

-From the ashes of agony comes humor and humility

1

In the dimly lit room I cautiously lifted the lid, the peppermints inside glimmering like hidden treasures. The clink of glass barely noticeable over the adults' laughter in the next room, I replaced it with the precision of a cat burglar. My mother's voice, threading through grandmas' den, spoke of a psychic's predictions captured on a cassette tape, stirring a whirlwind of curiosity in me.

Grandma's house, a testament to Frank Lloyd Wright's mid-century modern aesthetics nestled in St. Louis' suburbs, was usually my playground for adventures. The garage and loft, brimming with forgotten relics, and the creek bed, with its whispered secrets, usually captivated my imagination. But that day, the tape became my obsession.

I approached my mother, my voice quivering with feigned nonchalance, asking to listen to the tape. Her response, a stern 'absolutely not,' sealed its fate as my forbidden quest. I retreated, masking my burning curiosity with a shrug, but inside, a plan was already taking shape.

That night, the house slumbered as I tiptoed to my mother's suitcase, the zipper's whisper a thrilling sound in the silence. The cassette tape felt like a relic in my hands as I crept to the garage, the tape recorder my co-conspirator in uncovering the forbidden.

As the psychic's voice crackled through the speakers, a chill ran down my spine. The prediction about my future – a shadowy vision of me in a wheelchair – was unsettling yet vague. Disappointment mingled with a tinge of relief, the prophecy was not as earth-shattering as I had feared. I listened to the end, the tape whirring to a stop, leaving me with more questions than answers.

The prediction echoed in my eight-year-old mind, a distant storm on the horizon of my life. Yet, as life resumed its normal rhythm, the weight of the prophecy became a mere whisper in the dissonance of childhood, a riddle of the future wrapped in the enigma of the present.

2

The relentless shrill of my alarm at 6:00 AM shattered the silence of my dorm room, a harsh reminder of the day ahead. It was October 19, 1991, three weeks since my 21st birthday, and the reality of my new life at Rochester Institute of Technology was just beginning to sink in. Leaving Colorado State University's business program for a dream in imaging felt right, but this morning, doubts clouded my mind like the relentless rain outside.

The cold, wet morning mirrored my regret over last night's party - a decision now haunting me with just three hours of sleep. Rubbing my eyes, I could still feel the heavy air of cigarette smoke that had become a staple since my move to the East Coast. The shift from tobacco chewing, a habit I picked up in Colorado, to Marlboro Light cigarettes was supposed to be a fresh start, but now it felt like another ball and chain.

I coughed, a harsh, wracking sound that echoed in the empty room, and winced at the pain in my chest. Bronchitis had been my unwelcome companion since the move, yet another consequence of my choices.

Standing by the window, I watched the rain beat relentlessly against the pane. The rhythmic 'tap-tap-tap' seemed in sync with my throbbing headache. I checked my watch, 6:50 AM, and hurriedly grabbed my jacket. My mother's words from last night echoed in my mind, "Be ready at 7:00 AM in the parking lot."

The chill of the morning hit me as I stepped outside, the rain soaking through my clothes. I huddled under my umbrella, waiting. Time crawled by, each minute stretching longer than the last. I checked my watch – 7:05, 7:10, 7:15 – still no sign of her. My frustration grew with each passing moment, the cold seeping into my bones.

Finally, the familiar hum of a car engine cut through the rain. Relief washed over me as my mother's rental car pulled into view. "Hey, sorry I'm late," she said, her voice barely audible over the rain.

I jumped into the car, grateful for the warmth. We chatted briefly, my mother outlining her plan for the weekend – a cabin in the Finger Lakes region of upstate New York. Exhaustion clawed at me, and I suggested a detour to her hotel for rest, but she was intent on her plan. Resigned, I leaned back in the seat, the comfort of the car lulling me into a fitful sleep.

The journey was a blur of rain and half-formed dreams. I was dimly aware of a stop at a convenience store, my mother's voice mentioning coffee before I slipped back into unconsciousness.

Suddenly, chaos erupted. The sound of frantic knocking and muffled voices penetrated my slumber. "Are you okay?" they asked urgently. Irritated, I muttered, "Leave me alone, let me sleep," and darkness claimed me once more.

I awoke to an unreal sensation of floating. My eyes fluttered open to the sight of a cable hoisting me into a helicopter, its blades roaring overhead. A medic, her face etched with concern, told me I had been in an accident. I tried to process her words, but consciousness slipped away again.

When I regained awareness, I was in a hospital bed, a nurse standing over me. Confusion and defiance surged through me. "I need to get back to school," I insisted. Her response, gentle yet firm, stopped me cold. "You can't, Matt. You're paralyzed. You can't move your hands."

Disbelief turned to panic. I focused all my energy on moving my fingers, sure I could feel them obeying. But there was no movement, no sensation. Only the nurse's sympathetic gaze and her quiet, repeating words, "They're not moving…"

In that moment, my world shattered. The path I had been so sure of, the future I had envisioned, all lay in ruins. The realization that I was paralyzed, trapped in a body that no longer responded, it was overwhelming. Perhaps a turning point, the beginning of a journey I had never planned for – a journey into the unknown depths of my own resilience.

3

My mother, who had miraculously survived the accident with less severe injuries, was in a different hospital, hours away. The details of that chaotic day were foggy, but I remembered my father's desperate efforts to get me home. He had maxed out credit cards to arrange a medical jet for me, a testament to a parent's love that knew no bounds.

On that flight, amidst the hum of the jet engines and the occasional interjections of the male RN monitoring my vitals, I felt a sense of surreal detachment. My mother's presence was a comforting blur, her quiet strength a lighthouse in the storm of my pain and confusion. The flight was fraught with risk, at one point, I began to choke, my body rebelling against the trauma it had endured.

Arriving at Swedish Medical Center, I was immediately whisked to the Neurotrauma unit. The flurry of activity around me was a blur – visitors staring at me, doctors moving swiftly, nurses murmuring instructions, the cold touch of metal and the sterile smell of the hospital assaulting my senses. Surgeries were performed to relieve the fluid on my brain and stabilize my neck, a halo brace imprisoning my head in a rigid embrace. A piece of bone was taken from my hip to reconstruct my damaged cervical vertebrae.

During the surgery, something extraordinary happened. I found myself drifting out of my body, moving up through a tunnel of ethereal light. The experience was beyond words – a sense of peace and comfort enveloping me, a stark contrast to the physical agony I had been enduring. There was no pain here, no discomfort, just an overwhelming sense of well-being.

As I ascended, voices at the top of the tunnel beckoned me. "Relax, give up, you're done," they coaxed, their words a siren song tempting me to let go, but a part of me resisted, clinging to life.

I wasn't ready to leave. "I don't want to go," I found myself replying, my voice a mere whisper in the celestial expanse.

Their insistence grew, "It's okay, let yourself go." But I wasn't ready. Amidst the surreal peace, a thought flashed through my mind – a thought so vivid and absurd in that moment that it jolted me. "But there are so many hot women visiting me and I don't want to go!" I exclaimed, the absurdity of the statement echoing in the tunnel.

The voices laughed, a sound that was both comforting and mocking. And then, with a sudden 'zip', I was sucked back down, hurtling towards my body with an unrelenting force. The impact as I re-entered my physical form was jarring, a violent collision that snapped me back to reality.

During the aftermath of that out-of-body experience, I lay in the hospital bed, a new sense of purpose slowly taking root within me. The voices in the tunnel had offered release, but I had chosen to fight, to cling to the life that was so precariously hanging in the balance. It was a decision that would define my journey ahead – a journey fraught with challenges and discoveries, a testament to the resilience of the human spirit.

Interpretation of Near-Death Experience. Created using Midjourney AI.

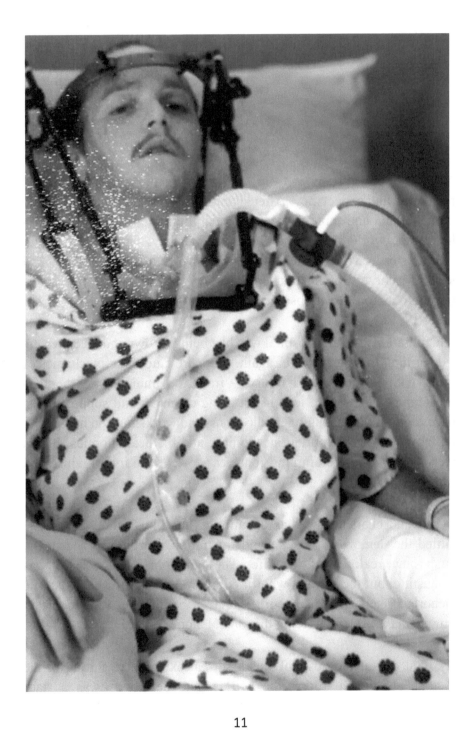

4

The day of my discharge from the hospital dawned with a mix of trepidation and expectancy. After six months – three of immobility due to pneumonia and three in rigorous rehabilitation at Craig Hospital – the outside world seemed like a distant memory. The hospital room, with its sterile whiteness and the constant hiss of the ventilator, had been my universe. The tracheotomy had robbed me of my voice, turning me into a silent observer of my own life.

Rehabilitation at Craig Hospital was like being thrown into deep waters and learning to swim all over again. We were taught the mechanics of living with a spinal cord injury – from the mundane to the life-threatening. There were lessons on using catheters and suppositories, discussions about managing medications, and workshops on navigating the labyrinth of transportation, funding, and medical supplies. It was overwhelming, like cramming four years of college into a whirlwind three months.

The mental challenge was as daunting as the physical. Every day, I battled the demons of despair and frustration, learning to accept the harsh new realities of my life. The emotional rollercoaster was exhausting, but the visitors who filled my room day after day kept me anchored. Their faces, sometimes blurred by fatigue, were constant reminders that I wasn't facing this ordeal alone.

My final day at the hospital was a surreal experience. Sitting in the doctor's conference room, the MRI image before us was a stark reminder of the fragility of life. The doctor's words, "There is no reason why you should be paralyzed," echoed in my mind, a haunting melody of hope and uncertainty. His cautious optimism about potential recovery was a thin thread to cling to, but in the depths of despair, even the slightest hope shines like a beacon.

Leaving the conference room, my wheelchair seemed like an extension of myself – a necessary part of my new identity. Every push down the hospital corridor was a laborious exercise, a constant reminder of my new limitations. The fluorescent green of the wheelchair, chosen to reflect a brighter aspect of my personality and a nod to my BMX biking days, now seemed like a small rebellion against my circumstances.

The journey home was a vision of past and present. Each familiar landmark was a whisper of memories, of a life that once was. As the car approached my parents' house, the sight of the newly installed ramp where the steps used to be was jarring. My childhood home, once a playground of adventures, had transformed into a fortress equipped to handle my new battle.

Inside, the house had undergone subtle yet profound changes. The laundry room, now a makeshift accessible bathroom, was a testament to my family's unspoken acceptance of my new reality. The familiar scents of home cooking and the sounds of life happening around me were both comforting and alienating. I was home, yet everything had changed.

As I maneuvered through the corridors of the house, each turn and each doorway was a negotiation between my past and present self. The laughter and chatter of my family, usually a source of joy, now felt like echoes from a world I was struggling to fit back into.

That night, as I lay in my new room, now equipped with medical aids and devices, the reality of my situation settled heavily on me. I was a

C5/6 quadriplegic, confined to a wheelchair, my independence curtailed.

Yet, amid the uncertainty and the grief for a life lost, there was a burgeoning sense of resilience. The journey ahead was daunting, but the outpouring of support and love from those around me was a lifeline. As I drifted off to sleep, the familiar sounds of my family's activities were a lullaby of normalcy, a reminder that life, in all its altered form, was still going on. And with that realization came a determination to not just exist, but to live – to find new ways to experience joy, purpose, and fulfillment in this uncharted chapter of my life.

5

The transition from hospital to home was a stark contrast to what I had imagined. There was no fanfare, no grand revelation – just a quiet settling into a new reality. I had naively hoped, somewhere in the recesses of my mind, that leaving the hospital would mean leaving the wheelchair behind. But there I was, in our old living room, now repurposed as my bedroom, the fluorescent green chair my constant companion still by my side.

The room, with its window facing west, offered a comforting view of our backyard. The sunsets were a daily spectacle, painting the sky in hues of orange and pink, a visual feast that momentarily took me away from my confined existence. The doors leading to the backyard and the garage were my gateways to the outside world, yet they also represented barriers I had to learn to navigate.

My first attempt at independence was a harsh lesson in physics and architecture. The ramps, hastily constructed by a now-absent contractor, were a crude solution – steep inclines without the necessary flat landings at the top. I recall one day, venturing out into the garage, the door clattering shut behind me. I hid behind a giant saw left by friends who had installed the wooden floor in my room. The embarrassment of being seen in my bright green wheelchair by the neighbors was too much to bear.

Trapped in the garage, I waited for my parents to return home, to help me conquer the incline that had defeated me. These early days were a constant battle against my new limitations, a frustrating dance of trial and error.

But it wasn't all despair. My father had bought me a computer with Windows 3.0, a portal to a new world that soon consumed my hours. I delved into various software applications, losing myself in the digital universe where my physical limitations didn't matter. Friends would come over, adding new programs, expanding my virtual playground.

One night, driven by a sense of rebellion, I pushed myself down the ramp into the backyard. The crickets were chirping, their rhythmic song blending with the rustle of leaves. I looked up at the night sky, a vast expanse of darkness sprinkled with stars. The Milky Way stretched across the sky, a celestial masterpiece that I had longed to see during my months in the hospital.

As I gazed upwards, a wild thought crossed my mind. I found myself silently pleading with the universe, with any intelligent life out there, to fix me – to offer a solution that the doctors on Earth could not. The absurdity of wishing for extraterrestrial intervention wasn't lost on me. In 1992, talking about UFOs or aliens could easily brand you as delusional, a label I wasn't eager to acquire.

So I kept these thoughts to myself, a secret shared only with the stars. Even in the privacy of my mind, I questioned my sanity for harboring such fantasies. Yet, in those quiet moments under the starlit sky, those thoughts brought a strange comfort. They were a silent acknowledgment of my deepest hopes and fears – a yearning for a miracle, for an escape from the reality that had become my life.

As the days turned into weeks, my room became both a sanctuary and a prison. The familiarity of the walls, the view from my window, and the routine of my daily life were comforting. Yet, there was an undercurrent of frustration, a constant reminder of everything that had changed.

I spent my days oscillating between hope and despair, grappling with the new identity that had been thrust upon me. The joy of being home was tempered by the challenges of navigating this new existence. The ramp outside my room, once a symbol of freedom, now felt like a metaphor for the uphill battle I faced every day.

But amid the struggles, there were moments of profound clarity. Looking at the stars, feeling the cool night air against my skin, I realized that life, in all its complexity, was still a beautiful mystery. My journey had taken an unexpected turn, but it was still my journey – a path filled with obstacles, yes, but also with moments of unexpected beauty and quiet revelations.

As I wheeled myself back up the ramp that night, a sense of determination settled within me. I might have been bound to my wheelchair, but my spirit was free to roam the vast expanses of my imagination. And in that realization lay the seeds of resilience – the understanding that while my body was limited, my mind was boundless, ready to explore new worlds, both real and imagined.

6

A few years later the wheels on my chair crunched over the asphalt, a stark contrast against the serene backdrop of the park. I felt a pang of frustration, battling with the all-too-familiar sensation of helplessness. In my mind, I chastised my body for its betrayal, but as I looked up at the azure sky, a whisper of determination silenced my inner turmoil. "Just one more lap," I murmured to myself, the words a lifeline in the vast ocean of my thoughts.

I remembered the days when running through this very park was as effortless as breathing. Now, each push of the wheels was a testament to my resolve, a challenge I faced head-on every other day. The memory of phone numbers I once dialed with ease, now elusive specters in my mind, served as a reminder of the journey I was on. My muscles ached, but there was a sense of accomplishment in that pain, a sign of the strength I was slowly, but surely, rebuilding.

Leaving the park's tranquility for the bustling suburban streets, I approached my home—a condo I had transformed into a semblance of a pirate ship. The front ramp, which I insisted be made of vertical planks, resembled the plank one might walk to board a ship. This feature, while initially met with skepticism from contractors, now stood as a proud testament to my independence.

Inside, the transformation continued. The walls were cloaked in black wallpaper, reminiscent of a ship's dark interior, while the windows were draped with white Roman shades, their appearance akin to sails.

The white wood floor, which I affectionately termed the deck, brightened the space where the dark walls ceased, creating an effect of lightness and openness.

Inside, my two companions, a Rottweiler, and a Bengal leopard cat, greeted me with a mix of enthusiasm and grace. We were an odd trio, bound by our shared space and the unique rhythms of our coexistence. The Rottweiler's protective nature and the Bengal's adventurous spirit had given me a window into a world different from my own, one where instinct and presence were everything.

That evening, as I settled in with my pets, the news droning in the background, I reflected on my journey. The years following my accident had been a whirlwind of adaptation, learning, and growth. I had rekindled my passion for creating through Photoshop, finding solace in the digital canvases that allowed me to express myself in ways I never thought possible after the accident.

My journey was far from over, each day presenting new challenges and opportunities. But as I sat there, in the condo I had adapted, surrounded by my unconventional family, I realized that this journey was not just about adjusting to a new normal. It was about redefining what normal meant to me, about finding strength in vulnerability, and about building a life that was uniquely mine.

The glow of the computer screen bathed the room in a soft light as I lost myself in the world of digital art. The clicks and hums of my machine were a harmony to my ears, a stark contrast to the quiet of the night. Each stroke of the trackball brought my ideas to life, images forming from the ether of my imagination, a process that always felt like magic.

My mind wandered back to the days of the dark room, the smell of chemicals, the red light, and the thrill of watching images appear on paper. Now, it was pixels on a screen, yet the excitement was the same. Creating art was not just a hobby, it was a part of my soul, a piece of what made me whole again.

The next morning, I awoke to the sound of the Rottweiler's gentle snoring and the Bengal's purr. We had our routines, the three of us, a dance of sorts that we perfected over time. Their presence was a constant reminder of the simple joys in life, a lesson in living in the moment.

I spent my days pushing the boundaries of what I thought possible. The wheelchair, once a symbol of my limitations, had become an extension of myself, a tool that granted me freedom. With strap-on weights and a standing table, I worked tirelessly to strengthen my body. The physical exertion was grueling, but with each passing day, I felt a surge of vitality coursing through me.

The culmination of my efforts came when I finally got behind the wheel of a Ford van. The sense of independence was exhilarating, the open road a canvas of possibilities. I remembered the first time my leg spasmed, causing my foot to slam on the gas pedal. My heart raced as I fought to regain control, a stark reminder of the delicate balance I navigated each day.

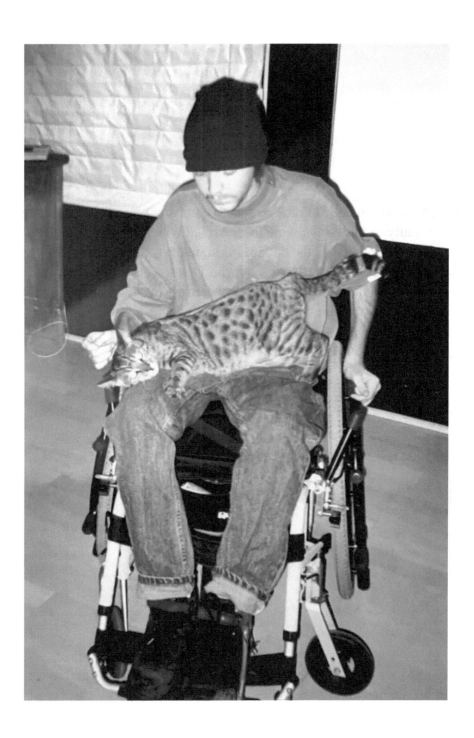

7

In time, a settlement from the rental car company provided me with an opportunity to build my own house. Armed with the knowledge I had gained from modifying the condo, I designed a space that was not just accessible, but a true reflection of who I was. The process was both challenging and rewarding, each decision a step towards creating a sanctuary that was uniquely mine.

Later as I sat in my custom-built home, I realized that these eight years had been a metamorphosis of sorts. Gone was the person who viewed life through the lens of what was lost. In their place sat someone who saw life for what it could be, full of potential and ripe with opportunity.

I had not experienced psychic awakenings or encounters with the unknown in these years. My focus was solely on rediscovering myself, on embracing this new chapter with open arms. Little did I know, as the new millennium approached, my journey was about to take an unexpected turn, one that would challenge everything I thought I knew about the world and myself. For now, I basked in the knowledge that I had not just survived, I had thrived.

8

The metallic saucer hung motionless in the sky, a surreal apparition against the backdrop of a clear August day. My heart raced with a mix of excitement and disbelief, the surreal sight rendering me momentarily speechless. "Can you all see that?" I finally managed to stammer out, my voice laced with awe and a tinge of uncertainty.

The warm August sunbathed the countryside in a golden hue, casting long shadows across the rolling hills of my mother's ranch. The air was fragrant with the scent of freshly cut grass and the distant, sweet aroma of hay. I was comfortably seated in the passenger side of my newly acquired millennium silver Toyota 4Runner, feeling a sense of contentment. The SUV, a perfect solution to my mobility needs, allowed me the freedom to explore with ease.

My brother was at the wheel, navigating the rugged terrain of the ranch with an expert hand. In the backseat, our mother and stepfather chatted idly, their voices a comforting background hum. We had been driving across the vast expanse of the property, a mixture of open fields and low grasslands, home to horses, alpacas, llamas, and a variety of other animals.

As we approached a canyon at the property's edge, the terrain became more challenging, but the 4Runner handled it with ease. The ride was smooth, the gentle purr of the engine a testament to the vehicle's power and reliability. We reached the canyon's edge, took in the breathtaking view, and then turned back toward the house.

It was on our return journey that it happened. I glanced up, expecting nothing more than the endless expanse of blue sky. Instead, I was met with an extraordinary sight—a metallic saucer, unmistakably a UFO, hovering silently above us. Its surface was smooth and reflective, almost blending into the sky but for the faint, dark halo that seemed to envelop it.

"Look! Up there!" I exclaimed, pointing upward using my elbow. My brother brought the 4Runner to a gentle stop, and we all gazed upward in stunned silence. The saucer was motionless, as if suspended in time, its presence both menacing and mesmerizing.

I felt a rush of adrenaline, my mind racing with questions and theories. The UFO was unlike anything I had ever seen or imagined—a perfect disc, with a strange blur around it, suggesting some kind of propulsion system I couldn't begin to understand. I thought of the camera resting on my lap, my first digital camera, but in the moment, I was too captivated to remember to ask the others to use it.

We sat there, in the middle of the ranch, staring up at the saucer for what felt like an eternity but was probably only a few minutes. Then, as suddenly as it had appeared, the UFO vanished. It didn't fly away or fade, it simply ceased to be, as if it had slipped back into whatever realm it had come from.

The rest of the drive back to the house was shrouded in a heavy silence. My family seemed reluctant to speak of what we had just witnessed, perhaps out of fear or disbelief. But I couldn't contain my excitement and curiosity. I was buzzing with thoughts and questions, the image of the UFO imprinted in my mind.

27

Interpretation of UFO sighting. Created using Midjourney AI.

Once home, I couldn't stop thinking about the encounter. My brother refused to discuss it, but I was already eager to dive into research. The possibility of extraterrestrial life had never been a fascinating concept to me, but now, having seen something so inexplicable, so otherworldly with my own eyes, I was consumed by the need to understand.

"Oh my God, I've just seen a UFO," I thought to myself, the reality of the experience both exhilarating and bewildering. It was a rare and extraordinary moment, one that few people ever get to experience. I knew then that this encounter would change the course of my life, propelling me into a journey of discovery and exploration that I could never have imagined.

9

As I sat in the quiet of my living room, the fading light of dusk casting long shadows, a book on Tibetan Buddhism lay open in my lap. I felt an intense pull towards the words, a deep yearning for understanding that went beyond mere curiosity. "Could this be the key to what I saw?" I whispered to myself, the memory of the UFO encounter still vivid in my mind.

The evening was serene, a gentle breeze rustling the curtains as I delved into the depths of Tibetan Buddhism. The house was quiet, the only sound the soft ticking of the clock on the wall. The book on my lap, opened to a detailed exploration of Vajrayana Buddhism, felt like a gateway to another world, one that might hold the answers to the questions that had been haunting me since that surreal encounter.

As a teenager, I had distanced myself from Catholicism, finding its teachings and rituals out of sync with my inner beliefs. The UFO sighting had reignited my spiritual quest, leading me down a path of exploration that was as unexpected as it was profound. Buddhism, with its emphasis on enlightenment and inner peace, seemed to offer a different perspective, one that resonated with my yearning for understanding.

The pages were filled with intricate descriptions of meditation practices, the pursuit of enlightenment, and cosmology that spoke of multiple realms of existence. The more I read, the more I found myself drawn into a world where the lines between the physical and the spiritual blurred. The rich history of symbols and imagery in Vajrayana Buddhism, especially those representing celestial beings, seemed to echo the mysteriousness of my UFO encounter.

One evening, I reached out to a respected teacher in Tibetan Buddhism. It was a bold move, asking a guru to come to my humble abode. To my surprise, he agreed. His visit was enlightening, opening my eyes to the principles of Buddhism and how I could incorporate them into my life.

For the next year, my days were filled with reading and contemplation. I delved into the Hinayana and Mahayana schools before finding myself engrossed in the teachings of Vajrayana. The possibility that these teachings could metaphorically refer to experiences like my own UFO sighting was both intriguing and baffling.

I remember sitting in my chair one evening, the room illuminated by the soft glow of a lamp, as I pondered the connection between the altered states of consciousness achieved through meditation and the otherworldly experience I had. The thought that my encounter could be intertwined with these ancient teachings was both exhilarating and disconcerting.

The journey was not easy. The more I explored, the more I realized how vast and complex the world of spirituality was. I had moments of doubt, times when the connection between my experience and the teachings seemed tenuous at best. The sound of the pages turning, a soft 'whoosh', was a constant in my quest for understanding.

Eventually, I reached a point where I had to acknowledge that my path in Buddhism was not leading me to the concrete answers I sought. There was a sense of resignation, a feeling of a journey unfinished, as I closed the book and set it aside. My gaze drifted to the window, where the stars twinkled in the night sky, a reminder of the vast and mysterious universe we inhabit.

I knew then that my search for understanding was far from over. The UFO sighting had opened a door to a world of possibilities, and though Tibetan Buddhism had not provided all the answers, it had set me on a path of exploration and self-discovery. With a deep breath, I rolled across my house, feeling a renewed sense of purpose. There were more paths to explore, more knowledge to gain, and I was ready for the journey ahead.

10

The room at the Colorado Free University, steeped in the scent of sandalwood and a palpable air of mystery, felt worlds away from the familiar confines of my daily routine. As I sat there, self-doubt coursing through me like a stubborn undercurrent, I muttered under my breath, "Let's see what this journey brings." But deep inside, I never expected the profound revelation that was about to unfold.

That morning had dawned bright and clear, the kind of day that carried a promise of new discoveries. I remember waiting for the woman who had responded to the Craigslist ad, her aura of enigmatic confidence both intriguing and slightly disconcerting. Her proposal to guide me through unconventional experiences — past life regressions, Reiki, and energy healing — dangled before me like a challenge, pushing the boundaries of my comfort zone.

We entered the session room at the Free University, a space that seemed to be an eclectic mix of a meditation hall and an old library. The musty smell of aged books mingled with the sweet aroma of incense, creating an atmosphere that was both alien and oddly comforting. A few other participants were already seated, their expressions a mixture of curiosity and serene anticipation.

The teacher, a large woman with a presence as magnetic as it was imposing, stood at the front. Her frizzy hair framed a face marked by a lazy eye, which somehow added to her mystique. She spoke with a voice that was both soothing and authoritative, weaving tales of souls traversing through time, reincarnating in countless lives over thousands of years.

Despite her captivating storytelling, I couldn't fully buy into it. I had already decided on my escape plan, a fabricated tale of being a 1920s baseball player. It was simple, believable, and it would keep me from sticking out in this group of earnest believers.

But as the room dimmed, swallowed by the growing shadows of the evening, and the soft strains of a hypnotic melody filled the space, something within me began to shift. The teacher's voice, now a hypnotic cadence, coaxed us into a trance-like state. I felt an unexpected wave of relaxation sweep over me.

In this altered state, my mind transported me far from the dimly lit room. I was suddenly above a vast mud ridden battlefield, a horrific yet strangely serene tableau spread out in the distance. The ground was littered with the casualties of war — fallen horses, soldiers in blue and gray, their lifeless bodies painting a stark picture of human conflict.

Sunlight bathed the scene in a surreal glow, and a little bird chirped somewhere close by, its melody strangely comforting amidst the desolation. Looking down, I saw my legs dangling, no longer confined to my wheelchair, covered in some heavy canvas or cotton leggings, ragged boots with toes exposed. Soldiers moved around, one stared up at me and spit. I was clad in a grimy uniform, a silent witness to the carnage of what I now realized was the American Civil War.

The return to the present was abrupt, the teacher's voice pulling us back like a tide receding from the shore. The tape player clicked off, snapping me out of the trance. As I recounted my unexpected journey to the group, the teacher nodded thoughtfully, suggesting that such intense and violent periods often leave the most vivid impressions on our souls.

Interpretation of past life regression. Created using Midjourney AI.

Rolling out of that room, the weight of the experience hung heavily on me. My skepticism had been replaced by a sense of awe and a deep curiosity about the mysteries of the human soul and its journey through time. The drive home was a blur, my mind replaying the vivid scenes of the battlefield, a stark reminder of the hidden depths of our existence and the unexplored territories of our consciousness.

11

Lying in bed, the morning light barely filtering through the curtains, I was jolted by my phone's urgent ring. My caregiver's voice crackled through the speaker, frantic and trembling with fear, "He's gone off the dam... I can't come in today." Her words hung in the air like a storm cloud, leaving me engulfed in sudden and unexpected chaos.

The day had started unremarkably, with the soft hum of the suburbs waking up outside my window. That tranquility was shattered by the call, a moment that felt like the ground shifting beneath me. My caregiver's words, laced with panic and despair, echoed in my mind as I lay there, immobilized not just by my physical condition but now by circumstance.

The immediacy of her crisis, a tragic accident involving her garage door repair man boyfriend, someone I had indirectly known through her stories, sent ripples of shock through me. This guy, who I had steadfastly refused entry into my home, had always been a looming, unsettling figure in the background of our conversations. His aggressive demeanor, something I had taken a stand against, now seemed to have culminated in this terrible moment.

My mind backpedaled as I tried to process the situation. She hung up abruptly, leaving me with more questions than answers. I attempted to call her back, then her mother, only to be met with the grim possibility that the man might not have survived. The realization that she would be absent for at least a week left me in a precarious position, my usual backup caregiver unavailable due to surgery.

The hours that followed were a blur of anxiety and frustration. I lay in bed, feeling a mix of concern for my caregiver and a growing sense of helplessness about my own situation. It wasn't until late afternoon that relief finally arrived in the form of another caregiver, who managed to free herself from her commitments to assist me.

When my caregiver returned to work, the air was heavy with unspoken words and emotional turmoil. She apologized profusely for the chaos her absence had caused, her voice trembling with the weight of her recent ordeal. I understood her pain but made it clear that such a situation couldn't happen again.

Then came the moment that still sends shivers down my spine. We were in the bathroom when she suddenly asked in a hushed, eerie tone, "Do you sense him here?" The air felt charged, heavy with an unseen presence. I didn't respond, unsure of how to articulate the strange sensation that had been lingering around me since the news of the accident.

The tension escalated when we moved to my bedroom. She began to scream, claiming she could smell his cologne, a sensory intrusion that seemed impossible yet palpably real. Then, the TV flickered on and off, its screen a dance of static and shadows. Her shouts filled the room, a mix of fear and plea for him to leave her in peace.

And then, as if to confirm our worst fears, the garage door began its mechanical ballet – opening and closing with no one in sight. My caregiver rushed outside to intervene, her movements quick and decisive.

After that night, the house seemed to take on a life of its own. Cold drafts wandered through rooms like lost spirits, and the TV continued its unpredictable performance, turning on and off at the most unexpected times. It was a period marked by an eerie sense of otherworldliness, a brush with the unknown that left me contemplating the mysteries that lie beyond our understanding of death.

This experience opened a door to a world I had never given much thought to before. It made me wonder if there was more to my existence, a hidden ability to connect with those who had passed on. Despite the initial fear, I found myself embracing this newfound curiosity, pondering the possibilities of what lies beyond, and what messages the departed might be trying to convey through these unexplainable occurrences.

12

The years weave an intricate web of connections in our lives, some so profound they leave indelible marks. Narine was one such person in my life. As I maneuvered the paintbrush with my mouth, carefully blending the oils on the canvas, each stroke was a reflection of the times we shared since her arrival in 1999. Her energy and resilience had colored my world, much like the vibrant hues I now spread across the canvas.

Narine, who initially claimed to be from Russia but later revealed her true roots in the blend of Armenian and Azerbaijani cultures, had a demeanor that was hard to forget. She was a blend of stern professionalism and heartwarming kindness, a duality that resonated deeply with me. Her story, unfolding over the years, added rich layers of understanding and empathy to our relationship, much like the layers of paint I was now applying to my artwork.

Her resignation in 2011, necessitated by back issues, left a void that was hard to fill. Her departure felt like losing a part of myself, a sentiment echoed in the somber tones emerging on my canvas. It was around this time that I stumbled upon the concept of 'quantum entanglement', the ability of one thing to occur in multiple places, jiving with my attempts to make sense of the extraordinary patterns I observed in my life.

In a twist of fate that seemed more than mere coincidence, Fadima entered my life about a year later. She, like Narine, had come from a former Soviet Republic and shared a similar demeanor. It was almost as if the universe had conspired to bring a reflection of Narine back to me. Fadima stepped into the role with the same quiet strength and commitment, her presence in my life becoming a comforting echo of Narine's.

The canvas before me bore witness to my contemplations, each stroke a testament to these remarkable parallels. And then there was Rachelle, a blonde, blue-eyed massage therapist from New Jersey who drove a black Jeep – her time with me was impactful, though brief. Her departure was followed by the arrival of Athena, strikingly similar in appearance, background, and even her choice of vehicle to Rachelle. It was these uncanny similarities that led me to ponder the idea of 'people templates' – a recurring pattern of personalities and characters in my life.

Working on the painting, I mused over these connections. Was it quantum entanglement at play, linking the lives of these individuals to mine in a mysterious dance? The concept, though complex, seemed to explain the improbable parallels that had woven through my life's narrative.

Now, as I continued my journey with Fadima and Athena, our shared Libra birthdays, one three days before mine and the other three days after, adding yet another layer of synchronicity. I couldn't help but marvel at the intricacies of these relationships. Each brushstroke on my canvas was a homage to these connections, a celebration of the inexplicable forces that draw our lives together.

In the solitude of my home studio, surrounded by my paintings, I often found myself lost in thought, contemplating the deeper meanings and connections that life presents. These relationships, these 'people templates,' were not just coincidences, they were threads in the vast, interconnected tapestry of existence, each one adding depth and color to the story of my life.

13

The click-clack of the keyboard echoed in my silent home office as I updated my will, a sudden, inexplicable urge guiding my fingers. It was the spring of 2014, and this compulsion to organize my final wishes felt both urgent and out of the blue. Little did I know this mundane act would soon take on a chilling significance.

I remember that spring day vividly, the soft sunlight filtering through the blinds as I sat before my computer. There was a strange sense of urgency in the air, an invisible force nudging me to ensure my affairs were in order. As I listed my final wishes, detailing everything from the fate of my cherished belongings to the songs I wanted at my funeral, a peculiar sense of foreboding settled over me. Once done, I tucked the paper in my safe, the sound of the door clicking shut as I pushed the strange feelings aside and carried on with my day.

Two months later, I found myself lying on the acupuncture table, the familiar scent of herbal oils mingling with the sterile cleanliness of the clinic. The acupuncturist, a man I had come to enjoy chatting with over the past weeks, had just left the room, leaving me alone with my thoughts and the quiet hum of the clinic.

Suddenly, a cold breeze swept over me, freezing despite the warm room. It was followed by a low, guttural, demonic-sounding murmur, its words indecipherable but its tone unmistakably menacing. I lay there, frozen, as I felt one of the needles from my upper back, where I still retained some sensation, dislodge and clatter softly onto the table.

I tried to rationalize it as nothing more than a draft and my imagination, but unease gnawed at me.

The acupuncturist returned, his movements efficient as he removed the needles and helped me transfer back into my wheelchair. It was then that I noticed my breathing had become labored, each breath a struggle. The ride home was a blur of discomfort and shallow breaths, my caregiver none the wiser to my internal panic.

Once home, I rummaged through my drawers, finally finding an old inhaler. Its hiss and the subsequent rush of medication brought temporary relief, but the fear lingered. By the time my evening caregiver arrived and I recounted the day's events, her concern was palpable. Reluctantly, I agreed to her insistence on going to the emergency room, driven more by fear than conviction.

We arrived at a small, standalone emergency clinic, its unassuming presence a stark contrast to the full-scale hospital a short drive away. I had chosen it for its convenience and hoped for a quick resolution. The doctor, after a CAT scan, delivered the shocking news, "Your little acupuncturist buddy has flattened your lung."

His words hit me like a physical blow. "OK, now what do we do about it?" I asked, trying to mask my growing anxiety. His response, a decision to insert a chest tube right there, sparked a tense exchange with the nurses. They protested, citing the clinic's limitations, but he was adamant, even dismissive of their concerns.

As he rummaged for supplies, his frustration was evident when he found only one chest tube, the wrong size. Despite the nurses' objections and calls for an ambulance, he proceeded, a flick of his tongue betraying his determination. I lay there, apprehensive, the nurses' worried expressions mirroring my own fears.

The moment he inserted the tube, I felt a rush of relief as my lungs expanded, but the concern didn't fade. In the ambulance, the EMTs' surprise and disapproval of the procedure performed in such a facility confirmed my fears – something could've gone wrong.

As the ambulance sirens wailed, cutting through the quiet night, I couldn't help but reflect on the eerie foresight of updating my will. The sense of urgency, the demonic voice during the acupuncture session, and now this – it felt like pieces of a puzzle falling into place, a chilling reminder of life's unpredictable nature.

14

As dawn's first light seeped into my hospital room, the quiet murmur of Swedish Hospital in Englewood, Colorado, was a stark contrast to the turmoil of the night before. The nurse's offer to raise my bed was a simple comfort, yet it heralded the beginning of a day I would never forget—a day when the fragility of life became all too real.

The morning had started innocuously enough. The nurse's routine question about breakfast and the promise of a visitor hinted at a day of recovery and perhaps some semblance of normalcy. However, the tranquility was shattered when my caregiver, who had stayed in the hospital hallway overnight out of concern, entered my room. Her reaction was immediate and visceral, her scream, a harrowing sound that pierced the morning calm, was followed by her horrified exclamation, "Oh my God!" as her gaze fell to the floor.

Before I could process her reaction, she fled the room, her distress echoing off the sterile walls. The nurse's subsequent entrance and swift exit, accompanied by a similar exclamation of shock, heightened the sense of impending crisis. Moments later, the room was awash in a flurry of activity as a 'code blue' was declared, summoning every available hand to my bedside.

The medical team's urgency was palpable, their faces etched with concentration as they explained the dire situation—the chest tube, had nicked an artery, turning my bed into a distressing scene of unchecked bleeding. As they scrambled to stem the flow, a lightheadedness enveloped me, my vision clouding with a white, plasma-like haze that obscured everything except the faces that loomed close to mine.

Amidst this surreal, milky veil, details stood out with unnerving clarity, a nurse's ponytail flicking through my blurred vision, her clear glasses frames leaving neon streaks in the plasma fog that filled my eyes. The room, once a place of healing, had transformed into a stage for a desperate battle for life.

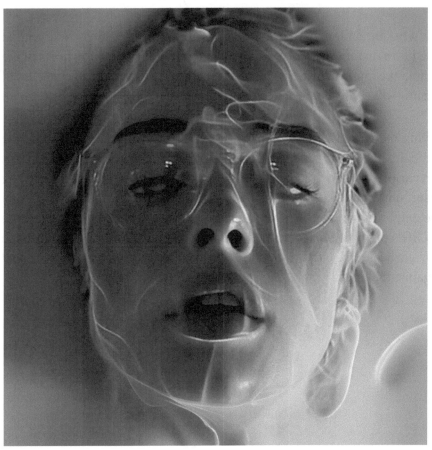

Interpretation of nurses' face through milky plasma. Created in Midjourney AI.

The air was thick with tension, punctuated by the rhythmic updates of my plummeting blood pressure. The numbers spoken aloud were a grim countdown, each one a step closer to the edge from which there might be no return. My usual low blood pressure was now a whisper from the void, the numbers chillingly low, a stark testament to the gravity of the situation.

In a moment teetering on the brink of eternity, one of the medical team voiced the stark reality: "This is his last chance, this is the oh shit moment." A tarp was thrown over my face in a gesture that felt like a prelude to a final farewell, the needle's plunge into my heart a desperate gambit to snatch life back from the precipice.

Slowly, miraculously, the fog began to lift, consciousness returning to me like a distant shore emerging from a mist. The frenetic efforts of the team, the multiple attempts to find a vein, the hovering specter of death—all coalesced into a singular, life-affirming moment of revival.

Lying there, on the cusp of what felt like a rebirth, the enormity of the ordeal washed over me. The experience was a stark reminder of life's precarious balance, a balance that had tipped wildly before righting itself under the skilled hands of those who refused to let it fall. In that hospital room, amid the chaos and the fear, I had journeyed to the edge of life's precipice and returned, carrying with me a profound gratitude for each breath, each moment, each beat of my heart that continued against the odds.

15

The chill of early spring did little to ease the heavy weight in my heart as I faced the inevitable. My loyal companion, a gentle black lab rescued from the shadows of a puppy mill, had reached the twilight of her years. The vibrant spirit that once filled every corner of our home was now a mere whisper, her once lively steps reduced to a struggle just to rise from her bed.

The dawn of 2016 brought with it a stark reminder of life's transient nature. My beloved Julie June Bug, whose timid yet sweet disposition had been a constant source of joy, was succumbing to the relentless march of time. For 11 years, she had been more than just a pet, she was my confidante, my shadow, my heart's companion through the highs and lows of life.

Her recent ailment, a stark contrast to the minor ear troubles we had overcome using Reiki, signaled a deeper, more irreversible decline. It was a poignant testament to the harsh truth that age spares no one, every creature inevitably facing its final chapter.

The decision to let her go was agonizing, each thought punctuated by a silent sigh of resignation. The drive to the veterinary hospital was a journey I had dreaded, each mile a step closer to an impending solitude I wasn't prepared to face. The weight of the decision pressed down on me, a burden no words could lighten.

In the sterile quiet of the veterinary room, the moment of farewell loomed large. When they brought her back from the examination, her joy at seeing me was a sharp pang of guilt, her eyes bright with the innocence of not knowing this was our last goodbye. The vet technicians gently lifted her onto the bench, positioning her so I could rest my hand, limited by paralysis yet full of love, upon her paw.

As the injection was administered, I watched her body relax, her struggle easing into a peaceful stillness. It was at that profound moment, as I braced for a wave of sorrow, that something extraordinary happened. An intense burst of energy surged through me, my vision dimming before being engulfed by the image of a majestic red phoenix, its cry piercing the solemn silence like a clarion call from another realm.

Interpretation of Julie's essence turning ethereal. Created in Midjourney AI.

This magnificent creature, rising with a primal screech, was a vibrant contrast to the somber finality in the room. The sensation was electrifying, an unexpected euphoria that filled the void of loss with a profound sense of continuation, of life beyond the constraints of the physical world.

In that instant, as I witnessed what I can only describe as Julie's essence transforming into something ethereal, I felt an indescribable connection to the cycle of existence. It was as if the veil between life and death had been momentarily lifted, revealing a glimpse of the transcendent journey that awaits us all.

The vision of the red phoenix, a symbol of rebirth and immortality, soaring upwards was a poignant reminder that in every ending, there is the promise of a new beginning. Julie June Bug's departure was not just an end but a transition to a state of being beyond my understanding, a continuation of her spirit in a form grander than I could have ever imagined.

As I left the veterinary hospital, the emptiness of her absence was tempered by the warmth of the experience. The profound energy and the vision of the phoenix provided a solace that words could not express. It was a testament to the depth of our bond and the enduring nature of love, a love that transcends the confines of life and death.

Rest in peace, Julie June Bug. In your final moments, you gave me the greatest gift—a glimpse into the mystery of what lies beyond, a reminder that love, in all its forms, is eternal.

16

The rhythmic clicking of gears shifting resonated through the crisp autumn air as I navigated my hand cycle around the quarter-mile track, the middle school a silent witness to my solitary journey. With each push and pull, my mind wandered, not to the physical exertion or the path ahead, but to a curious intertwining of lives that had puzzled me for years.

It was a cool November day, the kind that hinted at the impending winter, when I found myself on the familiar track near my home. Assisted by two caregivers, I was carefully transferred onto my hand cycle, a ritual that had become a cherished part of my routine. The track lay before me, an open invitation to push my limits and clear my mind.

As I started to pedal, the resistance of the 10th gear challenging my strength, my thoughts drifted to an event from earlier years. November 11, 2016, to be precise—a date etched in my memory not for its historical significance, but for the personal revelation it brought into my life. It was the day I met Andrea, the caregiver whose presence would unravel a tapestry of coincidences so profound, they bordered on the inexplicable.

Care.com had become my go-to in those days, a digital lifeline connecting me to a world of potential helpers. Among the various applicants, Andrea stood out not just for her qualifications, but for something intangible, an energy that seemed to echo a familiar presence—my mother, also named Andrea.

As my elbow shifted the gears down, easing the cycle's pace to navigate a curve, I reflected on the initial interview with Andrea. Her laughter at the mention of my mother's name was a prelude to a series of discoveries that would challenge my understanding of coincidence.

Over the six years of her employment, the parallels between the two Andreas unfolded like a well-scripted play. Both shared not just a name but a physical resemblance, with their short statures, brunette hair, and hazel-brown eyes. But it was more than just their appearance, their lives mirrored each other in ways that defied simple chance.

Pedaling through the track, I shifted the gears back up, the cycle's momentum mirroring the racing thoughts in my mind. Both Andreas had Midwestern roots near Des Moines, Iowa, a detail that could be dismissed as coincidence if not for the myriad other similarities. Their preferences, from disdain for dishwashing to a love for opera music, painted a picture of two lives inexplicably linked.

The most striking revelations were perhaps the most personal—their fathers' untimely deaths at similar ages, their significant others from different countries, both born in the year of the monkey, both unhappy with the lack of sharp cutlery in my kitchen, and even their shared hobby of pilot lessons. It was as if the universe was playing a game of cosmic matchmaking, drawing parallels so detailed and specific that they ventured into the realm of quantum entanglement.

Rounding the final lap, I slowed to a stop, my physical exertion a backdrop to the mental gymnastics of piecing together this puzzle. The younger Andrea, with her knowing laughter and elusive hints, only deepened the mystery, her presence a constant reminder of this unspoken connection.

As I was lifted from the hand cycle, the physical tiredness paled in comparison to the mental whirlwind the day's reflections had stirred. The story of the two Andreas, with their intertwined similarities, was more than just a curious anecdote, it was evidence of the mysterious forces that weave through our lives, connecting us in ways we may never fully understand. This encounter, this 'people template,' was a profound reminder of the unseen threads that bind us, a mystery that continued to unfold with each passing day.

17

The unexpected whirr of the ceiling fan breaking the silence had become a haunting reminder in my home, a mystery that began to unfold in the wake of a poignant trip to Home Depot with Carrie. That day, amidst the towering aisles laden with countless fixtures, a simple choice of a ceiling fan became the precursor to a series of eerie occurrences, immediately following the sudden loss of Carrie.

Our expedition to Home Depot had been a mission of practicality infused with Carrie's characteristic decisiveness. She led the way with a certainty that was both comforting and, at times, overwhelming. As we navigated the vast expanse of the store, she zeroed in on the most extravagant ceiling fan, its design a bold statement of industrial grandeur. "You need this one," she asserted, pointing upwards with an unwavering finger.

Despite my initial reservations, drawn to the more understated models, Carrie's persuasive argument about the suitability of the larger fan for my spacious, steam punk-themed room was hard to dismiss. Her insistence was palpable, and despite my desire for autonomy in the decision, I found myself relenting. "OK, let's get it and get out of here," I conceded, recognizing the blend of necessity and aesthetic appeal in her choice.

The installation of the ceiling fan marked a significant transformation in my room, not just in ambiance but soon in the unfolding of unexplained phenomena. Its presence became more than a mere fixture, it turned into a silent witness to an unseen realm, especially in the days following Carrie's tragic departure.

Carrie's death had come as a sudden shock, a loss that cast a long shadow over those who knew her. It was in the hours after her passing that the fan first exhibited its mysterious behavior, springing to life in the stillness, as if stirred by an unseen force. The light would flicker on without prompt, casting long, dancing shadows that seemed to echo the depth of our collective mourning.

The fan's activations became more pronounced, often occurring in the presence of certain caregivers, as if responding to the invisible threads of connection between us and someone who had passed. Each flicker of light, each spontaneous movement of the blades, was a whisper from beyond, a silent testament to the lingering presence of someone dearly missed.

The phenomenon reached a poignant climax one evening when a friend, who had also been close to Carrie, was in the room. The fan whirred to life, its movement more deliberate, the light casting a soft glow that enveloped us in a comforting yet eerie embrace. It was as if Carrie was reaching out, her spirit manifesting through the mechanical motions of the fan, a reminder of the bonds that death could not sever.

As the days turned into weeks, the fan's unpredictable behavior became a source of both fascination and unease. Its activations seemed to coincide with moments of remembrance, anniversaries of loss, or when conversations veered towards the ethereal. The air would shift, charged with an energy that defied logical explanation, as if the fan was a conduit for messages from a realm just beyond our comprehension.

Sitting beneath the fan, now a symbol of the unseen and the unexplained, I often pondered the profound connections that bind us to those we've lost. Was this a case of electrical quirks, or was there something more, a spectral communication facilitated by the fan? Each whirl of the blades, each flicker of light, was a haunting echo of Carrie's absence, a mechanical medium through which her presence was felt, leaving us to wonder about the mysteries that lay just beyond the veil of our understanding.

18

The sharp, unexpected twinge in my left wrist, a result of a seemingly innocuous mishap, marked the beginning of a journey that would delve into the realms of medical mystery and the unexplained. Despite the diminished sensation in that wrist, the pain was undeniable, and persistent.

The incident had occurred in the early months of 2018, a trivial twist of fate that I initially dismissed as a minor inconvenience. However, as days turned into weeks and weeks stretched into months with no relief, the constant throb in my wrist became a nagging reminder of my body's vulnerability. It was a discomfort out of proportion with what I understood about my own limited sensations, a riddle that traditional medicine seemed ill-equipped to solve.

Driven by a blend of frustration and curiosity, I began to explore alternative avenues for relief. The burgeoning field of stem cell therapy, with its promise of regeneration and healing, caught my attention. The idea of using my body's own resources to mend what was broken was appealing, a beacon of hope in the murky waters of chronic pain.

Armed with optimism, I secured an appointment at a reputable stem cell clinic, known for its long waiting lists and cutting-edge treatments. The clinic was a hub of innovation, where the potential of modern medicine seemed boundless. The doctors spoke of harvesting platelet-rich plasma (PRP) from my blood, spinning it down to its most potent components, and then injecting it back into the ailing parts of my body. The prospect was both fascinating and daunting.

As we delved into the possibilities, the doctor suggested an additional injection into my neck, near the site of my paralysis. The idea was speculative but intriguing, a shot in the dark that might illuminate new paths to mobility or, at the very least, offer some relief. Imaging was scheduled, a routine procedure that I anticipated would be just another step in this experimental journey.

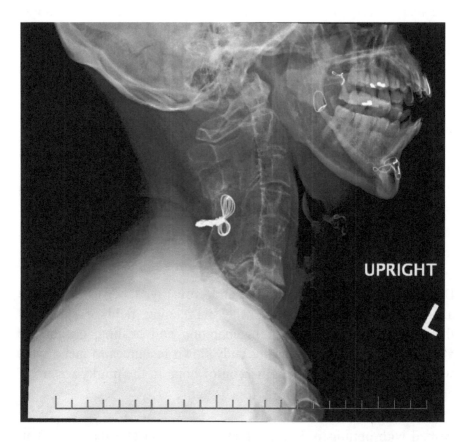

However, the follow-up consultation veered into the unexpected. As the doctor examined the x-ray's, her interest piqued by an anomaly near my C6 vertebrae. "What's this?" she inquired, her tone a mix of curiosity and concern. The zoomed-in image revealed a small, metallic object nestled near my spine, its origin and purpose a mystery. Her astonishment was echoed in my own confusion as I struggled to provide an explanation for something I was wholly unaware of.

The revelation cast a shadow of doubt over the proposed stem cell treatment, the doctor reluctant to proceed without understanding the nature of this metallic enigma. The cost of the procedure, a hefty $10,000 not covered by insurance, suddenly seemed a secondary concern to the pressing questions raised by the imaging.

Seeking answers, I turned to the nurse practitioner at Craig Hospital, a master of knowledge and reassurance in my ongoing journey with paralysis. Her nonchalant dismissal of the object as a likely remnant of past surgeries did little to quell my growing curiosity. Her laughter and assurance felt incongruous with the gravity of what the images suggested, leaving me adrift in a sea of uncertainty.

As time passed, my wrist gradually healed, the pain receding like a tide, leaving the mystery of the metallic object in my neck untouched, buried beneath the ebb and flow of daily life. Yet, the encounter with the stem cell clinic lingered in my mind, a thread loose and waving in the winds of unanswered questions.

My foray into the world of Ufology and alien encounters added layers of intrigue to the mystery. Tales of individuals with inexplicable metallic objects embedded in their bodies, often linked to otherworldly experiences, resonated with an eerie familiarity. The speculative leap from a medical anomaly to extraterrestrial interference was vast, yet in moments of reflection, I couldn't help but ponder the possibilities.

The enigmatic object in my neck, discovered almost by chance, remains a riddle wrapped in the mysteries of my own physiology and the vast unknowns of the universe. The doctor's parting words from years ago, hinting at the inexplicable nature of my paralysis, now echo with new significance, casting long shadows of wonder and speculation about the origins and implications of this tiny piece of metal hidden within me.

19

The hum of the podiatrist's office was a peculiar backdrop for contemplation, the sterile environment a stark contrast to the vibrant world of my imagination. Celebrating 27 years of navigating life in a wheelchair and my recent foray into the realm of independent fiction writing had imbued me with a sense of accomplishment and mystery, especially as I noticed the eerie echo of my written words in the fabric of my reality.

Late 2018 marked not just another year added to my life but also a milestone of resilience and creativity. Having adapted to the challenges of quadriplegia, I had found solace and expression in writing, crafting stories that flowed from my mind with ease, unencumbered by the need for physical setup or assistance. This newfound passion for storytelling was a liberating force, allowing me to weave narratives that transcended the confines of my physical limitations.

On that day, amidst the routine task of getting my toenails tended to— a chore my caregivers shied away from due to their gnarled, curvy nature—I found myself lost in thought. The clinical setting, with its antiseptic smells and the soft buzz of fluorescent lights, seemed miles away as I delved into a recent observation that bordered on the surreal.

My musings were interrupted by the podiatrist's careful ministrations, the sharp snip of his tools working meticulously. With each cut, I braced myself against the possibility of a spasm, my body a taut string waiting to snap. Yet, my mind wandered back to the curious phenomenon that had begun to unfold within the pages of my second novel, "Recurring Consequences."

The narrative had drawn heavily from a collection of past experiences and relationships, particularly an ex-girlfriend who had left a significant imprint on my life. In crafting a scene that mirrored a moment we had shared, I had unwittingly set the stage for life to imitate art. The fictional encounter, detailed with vivid imagery and emotion, had inexplicably played out in reality days after being penned. Her unexpected visit, her movements, and even her playful interaction with a painting in my hallway had mirrored my written words with unsettling accuracy.

This was not an isolated incident. As I continued to weave my tales, life seemed to echo my fiction with alarming regularity. A character's slow-driving habits, penned as a mere subplot, found its counterpart in one of my drivers, who, oblivious to my discomfort, trailed behind a garbage truck with no urge to overtake.

Each instance left me grappling with questions that blurred the lines between coincidence and something far more profound. Was I, through my narratives, somehow casting ripples into the future? Or had my intuition tapped into a well of precognition, my stories not so much creating as predicting the unfolding of events around me?

As the podiatrist finished his task, bringing me back to the present, I couldn't shake the sense of wonder and unease that enveloped me. The boundaries between fiction and reality, so clearly defined in the minds of many, had begun to fray at the edges in my world. Whether a conduit of creation or a seer of the unseen, the truth remained shrouded in mystery, the lines of my stories weaving through the tapestry of life in ways I could scarcely comprehend.

20

The unexpected stir of the ceiling fan in the quiet of my room felt like a whispered secret from beyond, a peculiar occurrence that coincided eerily with the news of Shelli's passing. While our friendship, born from a chance encounter and shaped by the shared trials of life in a wheelchair, had waned over time, this mysterious event seemed to bridge the distance between us once more, leaving me to wonder if there was more to it than mere coincidence.

In the warm embrace of early August 2019, the digital echo of Facebook bore the somber news of Shelli's departure from this world. Our paths had intertwined in an unusual manner, her minivan's persistent following of my routine outings with Julie June Bug leading to an unexpected bond. Shelli, from her spot in the passenger seat, had reached out with a warmth and curiosity that drew me in, despite our eventual realization that shared challenges did not necessarily forge a deep personal connection.

Our conversations, initially filled with the shared understanding of navigating life with spinal cord injuries, eventually gave way to the silence of faded contact, each of us retreating into our separate lives. Yet, the announcement of her passing, her journey ended not by her own hand but by the relentless advance of a medical complication, stirred a complex whirlwind of emotions within me.

That evening, as I retreated to the solitude of my room, a curious and inexplicable event unfolded. The ceiling fan, usually still and unobtrusive, began to move of its own accord. Its blades turned methodically, first in one direction then pausing before reversing, a silent, enigmatic dance that seemed to defy logical explanation.

The timing of this occurrence, so closely following the news of Shelli's passing, sparked a cascade of speculation within me. Could this be Shelli's way of reaching out, a final farewell imbued with a significance only she could impart? The fan's movements, unique and unreplicated since, suggested a presence or message, a guess that danced on the edge of the conceivable.

In my mind's eye, I envisioned Shelli, freed from the constraints that bound her in life, expressing her newfound liberation in a display of playful energy. The thought of her spirit, momentarily interacting with the mundane world through the ceiling fan, was a comforting speculation, a narrative that offered a glimpse into a realm where limitations dissolve and the spirit soars.

This singular event, whether a mere coincidence or something more, left an indelible impression on me. It invited me to entertain the possibility that in the vast, mysterious history of existence, there are moments when the veil between our world and the next thins, allowing for fleeting connections that defy explanation.

As the days passed and the gentle stir of the fan became a memory, the sense of Shelli's presence faded, leaving behind a poignant reminder of life's ephemeral nature and the enduring mystery of what lies beyond. In pondering the possibility of her final message, I found a sense of closure and a renewed appreciation for the enigmatic journey we all navigate, bound by the shared human experience yet touched by the inexplicable.

21

The eerie silence of my room was abruptly shattered by a distant, metallic ping, reminiscent of pinballs clattering, an uncanny prelude to an encounter that would defy explanation. November 2020, just a stone's throw from my 50th birthday celebration, had plunged me into a surreal chapter of my life, marked by a battle with Covid and an unexpected journey into the enigmatic world of UFOs with April, my newest caregiver.

The chill of November had settled in, a stark contrast to the warmth of my recent birthday celebrations. Yet, the festive air was quickly tainted by the onset of Covid, an invisible foe that forced me into the unwelcoming confines of a nursing home. The decision, made in a bid to protect my caregivers and their families, soon revealed itself to be a grave mistake. The care, or lack thereof, was a far cry from what I had envisioned, a harrowing echo of the aftermath of my 21st birthday when a car accident had first confined me to a wheelchair.

Desperation clawed at me, a need to escape the dismal treatment and reclaim some semblance of normalcy. It was April who became my hope in those dark days. Despite the clear risks, her willingness to brave the threat of Covid for a significant sum was a testament to the bond we had forged over our shared fascination with the unexplained— UFOs and alien encounters that had long captivated our imaginations.

Homecoming was a relief, a return to familiar surroundings, but it was our shared obsession with the extraterrestrial that truly marked the days that followed. Together, we delved into a marathon of documentaries, our screens illuminating the room with tales of close encounters and mysterious sightings. Our quest for truth was insatiable, each story fueling our belief in the existence of something beyond our understanding.

The discovery of Dr. Steph Greer's work on initiating close encounters of the fifth kind, CE-5, was a turning point, igniting a spark of excitement that was impossible to ignore. The $14 app, with its enigmatic tones believed to beckon UFOs, became our nightly ritual. Out on the deck, under the cold, starlit sky, we meditated, surrounded by the peculiar behavior of my black lab, Garland, whose sudden, erratic ground sniffing suggested an unseen presence among us.

Yet, it was on an ordinary morning, the sun casting its first light across the horizon, that the extraordinary unfolded. Three metallic orbs, like pinballs from some cosmic arcade, danced across the sky in a loose formation. Their slow, deliberate arc took them around the house, their gleam momentarily lost against the backdrop of the rising sun before reappearing with a playful flicker, a silent chuckle at our expense.

The realization that we had not captured this moment on our phones was a bitter pill to swallow, a missed opportunity to document the incredible. April's initial denial of the sighting was a puzzle, her agreement coming only after persistent coaxing, adding a layer of complexity to the experience.

The encounter, regardless of its fleeting nature, was transformative. It was a clear mid-morning, devoid of the shadows of dusk or the tricks of the night, when the orbs made their presence known. Their appearance, not during our nightly vigils but in the unexpected light of day, convinced me of their deliberate response to our calls.

Interpretation of Orbs occurring. Created with Photoshop.

This was no mere coincidence or earthly phenomenon masquerading as extraordinary. It was a genuine encounter, a response from the cosmos to the invitation we had extended. The experience solidified my belief in the existence of otherworldly entities, in the possibility of communication beyond the confines of our planet.

As I sat, reflecting on the encounter, the sense of privilege was overwhelming. To have witnessed such a spectacle, to have called upon the unknown and received an answer, was a profound affirmation of the vast, mysterious universe that surrounds us. This encounter, this moment of connection with the inexplicable, was a beacon of light in the shadow of my recent struggles, a reminder that life is an intricate container of experiences, some bound by the laws of nature, and others that transcend our understanding, inviting us to look beyond and wonder.

22

The still-fresh memory of the metallic orbs, a spectacle that had filled me with awe, contrasted sharply with the unfolding medical emergency. As I grappled with April's inexplicable lapse in memory regarding our shared encounter, I was thrust into a personal crisis that blurred the lines between earthly ailments and celestial interventions.

The week following our sighting of the metallic orbs was a disorienting dance of revelation and forgetfulness with April. One moment she would recall the event with clarity, only to slip into a fog of amnesia moments later, her memory flickering on and off like a faulty light. This cycle of remembering and forgetting added an eerie layer to the already mystifying experience we shared.

Amidst this bewildering aftermath, a more immediate and grave challenge emerged. A seemingly minor headache signaled the onset of a critical situation. My clogged catheter, a mundane aspect of my daily routine, had become a dire emergency, its malfunction leading to alarming symptoms that propelled us toward the emergency room with urgency.

The situation escalated rapidly once there. The removal of the catheter unleashed a flood of pent-up fluids, confirming the blockage and bringing me back to normal. It was the doctor's proposal for a CAT scan, meant to unveil any hidden issues, that morphed into a life-threatening ordeal. The failed attempts to establish an IV for the contrast dye were a prelude to a catastrophe. When the contrast was forcibly injected through an unstable IV line, it infiltrated my system, triggering a severe allergic reaction that constricted my airways and plunged me into a fight for survival.

As I struggled for breath, unable to voice my distress, the medical team's desperation was palpable. Their frantic attempts to secure a new IV mirrored the helplessness of the situation, my pulse dwindling to a mere whisper of life. The sense of déjà vu was overwhelming, a terrifying echo of past emergencies, so close to the precipice of death.

In that critical moment, as my consciousness waned and my life force ebbed away, the familiar sounds from the CE-5 app filled my right ear. These tones, which April and I had used in our attempts to reach out to the unknown, now seemed to reach back to me, a lifeline thrown across the chasm of the unknown. It was as if the entities we had contacted, through the same mysterious sounds that heralded their presence, were now intervening on my behalf, their ethereal melody a counterpoint to the chaos that surrounded me.

Before the doctor's second attempt at the IV, a profound sense of peace enveloped me. The constricted airways opened, my breath returned, and clarity dispelled the fog of panic. The medical team continued their efforts, oblivious to the miraculous recovery unfolding before their eyes. My insistent claims of "I'm fine" fell on deaf ears, their focus narrowed to the task at hand, unable to see the healing that had already taken place.

This brush with death, underscored by the spectral intervention, cast a new light on the encounter with the orbs and April's fluctuating memory. The orbs, April's erratic recall of the event, and the near-fatal episode in the emergency room wove together into a narrative that defied conventional understanding. The entities, it seemed, had not only made their presence known through the orbs but had also extended their reach into the very fabric of my existence, pulling me back from the edge with the same mysterious sounds that had once summoned them.

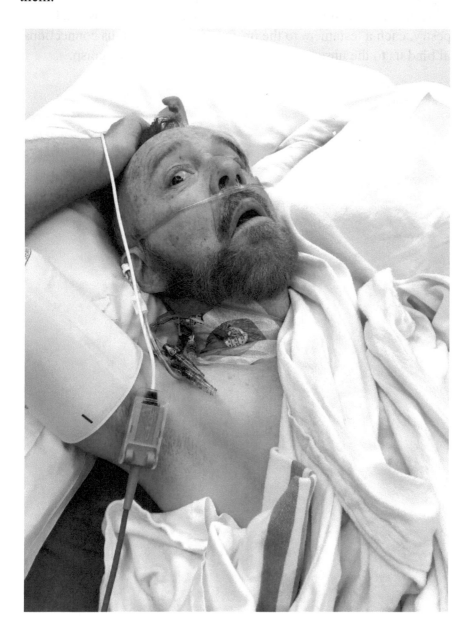

In the aftermath, as I processed the harrowing events, the interplay of life, death, and the enigmatic forces that intervened painted a picture of a universe far more intricate and interconnected than I had ever imagined. The encounter with the orbs, April's transient memory, and the inexplicable healing in the emergency room were threads in a larger tapestry, each a testament to the profound and mysterious connections that bind us to the unseen realms that lie just beyond our grasp.

23

The stillness of the night was shattered by a sound so startling, it seemed as though my entire house had come alive. This was no ordinary disturbance it was a clamorous uproar that left me bewildered and slightly unnerved. Amidst this confusion, the sight of my cat limping the following morning added another layer to the mystery, one that even the perplexing environment of the Peak Center and the rhythmic zap of the electrodes on top of my feet couldn't quite dispel from my mind.

It was a routine evening that turned peculiar in early November 2022, the tranquility of my home violently disrupted by a noise that defied logical explanation. The sound, reminiscent of a colossal drawer of silverware being hurled across the wood floor, echoed through the corridors with such ferocity that it jolted me awake, my heart racing in the deafening silence that followed.

The aftermath of the chaos was as crazy as the incident itself. Expecting to wake to a scene of domestic upheaval, I was met instead with the ordinary calm of my household, the anticipated disorder nowhere to be found. This inexplicable event was compounded the next morning by the sight of my cat, previously agile and unencumbered, now dragging his hind legs in a pitiful display of sudden affliction.

As I navigated the day, the residue of the previous night's enigma lingered, a curious blend of confusion and intrigue coloring my thoughts.

The incident became a focal point of conversation during my rehabilitation session at the Peak Center, where the Arjo walker and the Bioness L300 had become instrumental in my quest for mobility. Here, amidst the hum of machines and the focused presence of physical therapists, I found a semblance of normalcy, a contrast to the baffling occurrence at home.

Natalie, my physical therapist, sensing my preoccupation, inquired about the source of my distraction. In response, I ventured into the tale of the nocturnal disturbance, describing the jarring sound that had pierced the quietude of my home, its volume and intensity unlike anything I had ever experienced. The peculiar behavior of my cat, which coincided with the event, added a layer of intrigue to the story, its sudden lameness as unexplained as the noise itself.

The recounting of the event in the safety of the Peak Center, with the Arjo walker supporting my frame and the Bioness L300 combined with electrodes shocking the top of my feet to harness my reflex response and deliver movement in my legs, provided a stark contrast to the unsettling mystery that lingered in my mind. The sound, so vivid and jarring in my memory, was a mystery that neither I nor my caregiver that morning could solve, a topic that spurred curiosity and a slight edge of apprehension.

Even more baffling was the reaction of my renters occupying the walkout basement apartment downstairs, who, despite typically being oblivious to the sounds of my distress, had been roused from their slumber by the clamor, a testament to its undeniable reality. This shared experience, coupled with the lack of physical evidence to account for the commotion, deepened the mystery, leaving us all to ponder the source of such a disturbance.

As I continued with my rehabilitation, the memory of that night remained a curious footnote in my journey, a moment of inexplicable disruption in the rhythm of my daily life. The sound, the cat's temporary ailment, and the absence of any tangible cause were enigmas that weaved themselves into the fabric of my experiences, a reminder of the unpredictable and often unexplainable nature of our existence.

24

The click of my computer mouse echoed in the silent room as I launched my quest on Care.com, my digital lifeline for sourcing caregivers. The first profile to catch my eye was Sidney's, her image radiating vitality with a protein shake in hand, a promising possibility in the daunting task of assembling a team capable of navigating the complexities of my quadriplegic life.

The dawn of 2022 brought with it the pressing need for new caregivers, a challenge that had become all too familiar in the years following my injury. The process, though routine, was fraught with the uncertainty and hope that accompanies the search for someone to share in the most intimate details of daily life. Sidney's profile stood out amidst the sea of candidates, her aspirations of nursing, her background in personal training, and her passion for nutrition painting the picture of an ideal match.

Adhering to my tried-and-true method, I crafted a message detailing my needs, the hours, and the compensation, casting it into the virtual sea of Care.com in hopes of finding the right fit. This approach, while impersonal, was a necessary strategy in the unending cycle of hiring and training that had become a staple of my existence. The reality of my situation was a constant balancing act, juggling the roles of employer, manager, and patient, all while striving to maintain a semblance of normalcy in a life altered irrevocably by spinal cord injury.

The response from Sidney, along with four others, was a glimmer of hope in the arduous process. I scheduled interviews, each a potential step toward regaining the stability that caregiving turnover so often disrupted. The day of Sidney's interview arrived with the usual mix of anticipation and skepticism. My preparations were minimal, relying more on intuition and first impressions than on a list of predetermined questions.

Sidney's timely arrival was the first sign of her reliability, her well-maintained car an added assurance of her dependability. These initial observations were crucial, forming the foundation of my assessment before we even exchanged greetings. Upon opening the door, Sidney's presence was immediately reassuring—her energy, her eagerness to work, and her alignment with my schedule needs were palpable.

The interview, if it could be called that, was less a formal interrogation and more an exchange of energies, a mutual assessment of compatibility. Sidney's vitality and readiness to engage with the responsibilities of the role resonated with me, offering a sense of ease in the decision-making process. Her openness to the unique challenges of caregiving in the context of quadriplegia, coupled with her flexibility to accommodate my medical appointments, solidified my choice.

The administrative formalities that followed—contract signing, tax documentation, and the exchange of personal identification for payroll purposes—were a swift conclusion to our meeting. Sidney's departure left me with a rare feeling of contentment, a hope that perhaps this time, the fit would be right, that the revolving door of caregivers might pause, however briefly, allowing for a period of stability and mutual growth.

In hiring Sidney, I had not just filled a vacancy, I had potentially welcomed a new ally in my journey, a partner in navigating the intricate dance of life with a spinal cord injury. The prospect of dependable assistance, combined with the promise of shared interests in health and fitness, painted a hopeful picture for the days ahead, a reminder that even in the face of relentless challenges, there are moments of connection and possibility that sustain us.

25

The hum of the van engine mingled with the familiar sights of the neighborhood as I directed Sidney down memory lane, an impromptu detour that unwittingly bridged the gap between past and present. Little did I know that this casual drive would unravel a connection so profound, it would leave me pondering the serendipitous threads that weave the tapestry of our lives.

Sidney had been more than just a caregiver over the eight months we worked together, she was a companion on my journeys to personal training, a confidante during doctor's visits, and a reliable presence on the nights she helped me settle into bed. One sun-drenched afternoon, as we made our way back from an appointment, I felt a pull towards the past and suggested we take an alternate route home.

As we drove past the townhome where I had lived over two decades ago, nestled on a serene golf course and flanked by a picturesque reservoir, a flood of memories washed over me. I shared with Sidney the camaraderie of that community, how neighbors became friends and, in my case, an extended family that transcended mere proximity.

I reminisced about some of the young men from the neighborhood, close in age to me, who had once integrated me into their lives with a seamless ease that was rare and precious. We had shared nights of youthful revelry, their assistance in getting me home and into bed afterward granting me a taste of freedom that was both exhilarating and normalizing.

It was during one such night out that a fleeting encounter with a blonde woman had sparked a playful challenge between me and one of my friends. The outcome of that challenge had faded into the background of my life's ongoing narrative, a seemingly inconsequential ripple in the vast ocean of interactions that define our existence.

However, as Sidney and I continued our working relationship, one evening her sudden exclamation pierced the comfortable silence that had settled between us. Her excitement was palpable, her words a jumbled rush that hinted at a revelation so unexpected it momentarily suspended my ability to comprehend. "I almost forgot to tell you! Matt, you know my grandma, my mom, my dad, and my uncle," she declared, her enthusiasm painting her face with an intensity that demanded my full attention.

The pieces of the puzzle began to fall into place as she unveiled the astonishing truth, she was the very child conceived from the union of my friend and the blonde woman from that long-ago night. The realization hit me with the force of a tidal wave, a confluence of past and present that defied probability and logic.

The revelation that Sidney, whose path had crossed mine in such a mundane yet essential capacity, was intrinsically linked to a chapter of my life that I had filed away in the archives of my memory was staggering. It was a testament to the mysterious and intricate ways in which our lives intertwine, a reminder that the people we meet and the connections we forge, no matter how fleeting, can ripple through time and reemerge in the most unexpected ways.

As I processed this incredible twist of fate, I couldn't help but marvel at the cosmic dance that had brought her into my life, not just as a caregiver, but as a living bridge to a past that I had cherished and let go. The world, indeed, works in mysterious ways, its mysteries unfolding in the connections that bind us, often hidden in plain sight, waiting for the right moment to reveal the strangeness of our interconnected lives.

26

The sharp pang of pain that seized me that February afternoon was a prelude to an ordeal that transcended the bounds of my physical existence. Amidst the turmoil of a world grappling with the surreal reality of UFOs and a Chinese spy balloon in US airspace, I was thrust into a battle for life, one that would lead me to the brink of death and beyond, to a realm where the rules of our world no longer applied.

The discomfort started as a mere nuisance, a subtle whisper that something was amiss. By dusk, it had crescendoed into an agony that bent me double, a clear sign that this was no ordinary affliction. In my haste for relief and a misguided attempt to save time, I sought help at the small-scale emergency room I had sworn off after the previous mishap. The familiarity of the place did little to ease my growing apprehension as the pain intensified, a foreboding sense of déjà vu clouding my judgment.

The initial diagnosis was as mundane as it was misleading—a bladder infection. Yet, as the hours ticked by and my condition deteriorated, the true gravity of my situation came to light. Sepsis, the word echoed through the sterile corridors of the hospital, a chilling verdict that marked the beginning of an arduous battle. The prospect of enduring days tethered to IV antibiotics was daunting, yet it paled in comparison to the journey I was about to embark on.

On the third day, under the care of a nurse who claimed expertise with quadriplegics, my trust in her knowledge was put to the test. Her suggestion to use a sticker anchor for my catheter, despite my protests from previous adverse experiences, was a decision that would have dire consequences. Unbeknownst to me, she proceeded with her plan, an oversight that would soon plunge me into an abyss.

As the day wore on and I succumbed to exhaustion, my dreams became a gateway to another reality. The onset of autonomic dysreflexia in my dream was a terrifying signal, a desperate plea from my body that something was terribly wrong. Yet, I was trapped in a slumber that was more than sleep, ensnared in a realm that defied description.

This otherworldly place was shrouded in darkness, yet alive with purplish geometric structures that exuded a calmness alien to our world. The arrival of the Falcons, creatures of breathtaking beauty with their vast purple wings, heralded a journey through a landscape that radiated bliss. The cartoon-like insects that greeted me, their joy infectious, were a stark contrast to the peril my body faced in the waking world.

It was in this serene yet surreal landscape that I found a peace I had never known, a contentment that made the thought of returning to my physical existence unbearable. The path leading to a mysterious cave, the procession of people drawn to its depths, promised answers and an escape from the pain that had been my constant companion.

Yet, reality has a way of reclaiming its own. The frantic buzz of the call button, the rush of nurses, and the alarming spike in my blood pressure were a rude awakening from the tranquility of that other place. The discovery of the kinked catheter, a result of the nurse's well-intentioned but misguided intervention, was the key to unraveling the mystery of my condition.

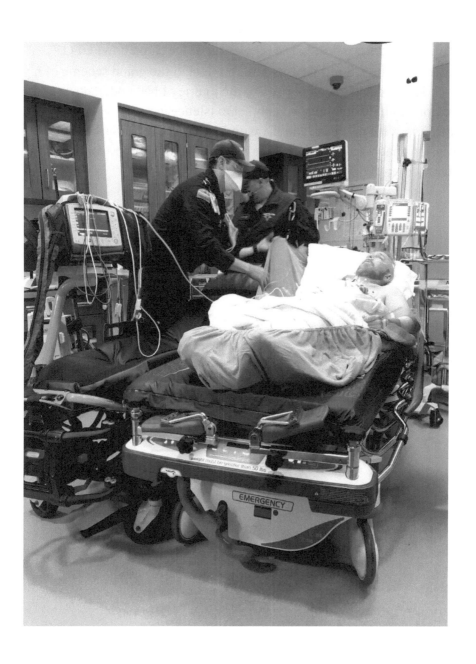

As my body slowly reclaimed its equilibrium, the memory of that ethereal journey lingered, a vivid reminder of the thin veil that separates life from death. The revelation of the Superbowl UFO downed by the US military, a mere footnote in the grand scheme of my experience, paled in comparison to the journey I had undertaken. In the face of death, I had glimpsed another existence, a realm where pain and suffering were no more, and the wonder of discovery was boundless— a vision that would forever alter my perception of the world and my place within it.

27

The clack of marble under my wheelchair wheels echoed like a metronome through the opulent lobby, marking my passage through time and space to meet Kevin, my steadfast financial advisor. Our annual post-Super Bowl meeting, a tradition spanning 26 years, was a ritual of resilience, especially poignant this year as I emerged from the shadows of the recent sepsis scare.

The grandeur of the investment firm's Italianate headquarters, with its marble expanse and imposing dome, never failed to impress, yet it was the familiarity of the routine that grounded me. My early arrival, the brief exchange with the receptionist, and the anticipation of Kevin's arrival were all part of a well-rehearsed dance, one that provided a comforting sense of continuity amidst life's uncertainties.

Kevin's timely appearance, always the epitome of professionalism, signaled the start of our annual financial review. As we settled into the conference room, the weight of the past week's medical ordeal began to lift, replaced by the gravity of assessing and planning my financial future.

The meeting unfolded with Kevin's characteristic precision, his analysis and recommendations laid out with the clarity that had guided my financial journey for over a quarter of a century. Yet, as he delved into the intricacies of portfolio adjustments and asset reallocations, my mind began to drift, not out of disinterest but toward a fascinating observation that had captivated me recently.

Amid Kevin's discourse on tax-exempt bonds and equity allocations, I found myself reflecting on the uncanny patterns revealed by the photo memories on my smartphone. Each morning, the app presented images from the same calendar day in previous years, unveiling a mosaic of recurring events that was both mundane and mesmerizing. Hawks perched in the backyard tree, the same outfit donned unwittingly on this day across different years, and social gatherings that seemed to favor certain dates had all been captured by the unassuming lens of my phone.

This digital tapestry, woven from the threads of past and present, offered a silent testimony to the rhythms that underpin our lives. It was a reminder that amidst the flux of health scares and financial planning, there exists a subtle order, a pattern of recurrence that binds the history of our existence.

As Kevin wrapped up the meeting, outlining the steps for the year ahead, I was struck by the parallel between his meticulous financial planning and the unwitting patterns captured in my photos. Both were narratives of my life, one measured in assets and projections, the other in pixels and memories, each frame a marker of time's passage.

Emerging back into the marble lobby, the resonance of our meeting mingled with the broader contemplation of life's patterns. The ritual of these financial reviews, set against the backdrop of recurring images and events, was a poignant reminder of the cycles that shape our existence. It was a moment to acknowledge the interplay of chance and design, the unexpected harmonies that emerge in the melody of life. As I waited for my driver, the echoes of the past mingled with the plans for the future, a symphony of continuity and change that underscored the enduring mystery of the patterns that define us.

28

The buzz of anticipation that ran through me as I prepared to share my orb encounter and emergency room experience was palpable. For years, I had kept the story close, shielded by silence from potential ridicule. But as the narrative around extraterrestrial phenomena shifted in the public eye, my resolve strengthened. The time had come to break my silence, drawn by a world increasingly receptive to the mysteries of the cosmos.

July 2023 marked a turning point, a moment when the ember of my desire to speak out transformed into a blazing need for acknowledgment. The orbs, the mysterious sounds, and the inexplicable guidance in the emergency room had been my silent companions, experiences too profound to remain unshared. Yet, fear of disbelief and the stigma of the unknown had kept me silent, a prisoner of my own experiences.

The Super Bowl UFO shootdown incident, with its dramatic confrontation between the known and the unknown, seemed to crack the door open to a world where discussions of otherworldly civilizations were no longer confined to the fringes. It was against this backdrop that I found MUFON, Mutual Unidentified Flying Object Network, an organization dedicated to the investigation of the unexplained aerial phenomena that had become an integral part of my life.

The podcast hosted by the Colorado contact of MUFON became my window to a community that dared to believe, to question, and to seek the truth. Her voice, a guide for those like me, held the promise of an audience ready to hear my story. The scheduled call, set three weeks into the future, was a date with destiny, a chance to finally voice the encounters that had silently shaped my worldview.

As the appointed time approached, I sought solace in meditation, my gaze fixed on the world outside, a world oblivious to the internal tumult of my revelations. It was then, in the quietude of my preparation, that a stark, unbidden warning pierced my calm, "Don't tell that woman anything!" The message, so clear and commanding, jolted me. It was neither my thought nor my fear, it was something else, an admonition from an unseen advisor.

Yet, driven by the need to share, to validate my experience, I chose to dismiss the warning. The call, once connected, revealed a reality far removed from my expectations. The skepticism in her voice was palpable, her demeanor dismissive, as if my story was but a drop in the ocean of encounters she had catalogued. Her attempts to minimize my experience, to categorize it as just another sighting in a state known for its celestial visitors, left me feeling diminished, my extraordinary encounter reduced to a mere statistic.

Her revelation that my home lay in proximity to a hotspot of UFO activity was intended to demystify my experience, yet it only deepened the enigma. The dismissal by someone I had hoped would understand was a bitter pill, yet it opened a door to a deeper exploration of the messages and insights that seemed to reach me from beyond the veil of our reality.

It was in the aftermath of this disheartening interaction that I found solace and resonance in Chris Bledsoe's narrative, "UFO of God." His ordeal with the very organization I had approached, MUFON, unfolded like a mirror to my own, a chilling reflection of misplaced trust and shattered expectations. Bledsoe's journey, marked by polygraph tests at the behest of the FBI and a subsequent unraveling of his reputation, painted a stark picture of betrayal. The organization, once a bastion of hope, became the architect of his despair, exposing him and his family to unwarranted scrutiny and danger.

This revelation was a clarion call, a stark reminder of the precarious path I tread. Bledsoe's experience, paralleling my own albeit on a different scale, underscored the potential perils of seeking allies in a realm rife with skepticism and hidden agendas. The warning I had so readily dismissed was now a prophecy fulfilled, a cautionary tale of the fine line between seeking understanding and falling prey to the plans of those cloaked in the guise of support.

Emboldened by this epiphany, I steered my quest for connection and understanding back into the realm of personal exploration. The phenomenon, once an external pursuit, became an inward journey, a quest for knowledge untainted by the biases and motivations of external entities. My experiences, unique and profound, demanded a stewardship that was personal and protective, a path forged in the solitude of my contemplation and the sanctity of my own understanding.

In this new chapter, I embraced the role of the solitary explorer, a voyager in the vast expanse of the unknown, guided by the internal compass of my intuition and experiences. The orbs, the sounds, and the whispered guidance in moments of peril were now jewels in the crown of my personal odyssey, facets of a truth that was mine to explore and cherish. The journey ahead was mine alone, a pilgrimage in the realm of the unknown, fortified by the lessons of the past and the boundless potential of the unseen future.

29

Under the vast expanse of the summer sky, the hum of the CE 5 Crop Circle sounds filled the air around me, a sonic bridge to the unknown. It was a leap into the abyss of the unexplained, spurred by tales of entities dwelling in dimensions just beyond our perception. As I sat there, the question "Can you fix me?" echoed in my mind, a plea cast into the cosmic void, not fully prepared for the response that would challenge my understanding of reality and self.

The concept of unseen beings, entities that coexist with us in a realm just beyond our senses, had always been a tantalizing notion. When the podcast aired that summer of 2023, discussing the potential of such beings and their interaction with those who've brushed against the veil of death or dedicated themselves to the depths of meditation, it resonated with me. It was as if the universe had laid out a path specifically for me, someone who had navigated the shadowy borders of life and death more than once and found solace in the quietude of meditation. "That's you, my friend! Let's go!" I affirmed to my reflection, a spark of resolve igniting within.

Armed with curiosity and the haunting tones associated with the CE 5 encounters, I ventured onto my deck, the open sky above me serving as the canvas for my experiment. The question was simple yet profound, "Can you fix me?" I asked, repeating it thrice into the night, half-expecting the silence to swallow my words without reply.
The response, when it came, was not through a voice or a sign, but a clear, unbidden thought that pierced my contemplation, "We cannot fix

94

you, we can only help you." The clarity and suddenness of the message left me stunned, my skepticism momentarily overshadowed by the sheer audacity of the experience. It was a moment of revelation, not the answer I had hoped for, but an acknowledgment of my plea from a source undefined and mysterious.

This encounter, brief as it was, marked a turning point in my journey. The realization that these entities, whatever they might be, could not offer the restoration I sought but instead proposed a subtler form of assistance, was both sobering and enlightening. It echoed my experience in the emergency room, where, amidst the chaos and uncertainty, I had felt an inexplicable sense of guidance, as if unseen hands steered the course of events in my favor.

Embracing this new role as an observer, I began to attune myself to the nuances of life, to the possibility of intervention by forces beyond our understanding. This shift in perspective was not just about looking for miracles or seeking answers in the unknown it was about acknowledging the profound interconnections that bind us to the cosmos, to each other, and to the myriad of entities that may share this journey with us, seen or unseen.

30

The sharp whirr of the paper shredder, devouring the old addendum to my will, was a stark reminder of the ever-present dance with fate. Little did I know that this act, so mundane yet profound, was a prelude to an adventure that would skirt the edges of disaster, challenging the very essence of premonition.

It was a crisp September morning when the impulse to revise my will surged through me with an urgency I couldn't ignore. The task, once completed, left me with a sense of closure, yet the ripples of change it set in motion were far from over. The new document, now resting in my safe, bore minor yet significant alterations—a testament to the evolving landscape of my relationships and preferences.

Days later, a message from Tim Burr, a fellow quadriplegic, and the visionary behind Return to Dirt, presented an opportunity that was both exhilarating and daunting. The offer to venture into the wilderness on ATV four-wheelers was a call to adventure, a chance to break free from the confines of routine and embrace the raw beauty of Glenwood Springs.

Mr. Fish, a longtime ally and jack-of-all-trades, was my chosen companion for this journey. His agreement to accompany me was a relief, his presence a guarantee of both practical support and spirited camaraderie. Our plan was set—a night's stay at a hotel to ensure we were primed for the day's adventure.

Yet, as the departure loomed, a shadow of unease began to cloud my excitement. An instinctive whisper, subtle yet insistent, urged caution, suggesting a deviation from our usual travel arrangements. My proposition to rent a vehicle, to secure a safer seating arrangement, was met with resistance from Mr. Fish. His concerns over cost and convenience overshadowed my nagging apprehensions, leading me to reluctantly categorize my fears as mere paranoia.

The journey into the heart of the Rockies was a visual spectacle, the majesty of the mountains a stark contrast to the growing tension within me. Glenwood Canyon, with its breathtaking heights and narrow margins, was a stretch I approached with a mix of awe and apprehension.

It was there, at the peak of the pass, that my fears materialized in a moment of sheer terror. As Mr. Fish unexpectedly switched lanes, the gravitational pull and my unanticipated spasms conspired against me. The Velcro belt, my only anchor, gave way with a resounding rip, propelling me towards him with a force that defied my attempts at control.

The ensuing seconds were a blur of adrenaline and fear. My body, draped over Mr. Fish and the steering wheel, was at the mercy of his strength and composure. His unwavering focus on the road, even as I lay across him, was the thin line that separated us from a fatal plunge into the canyon's depths.

Once the immediate danger had passed and I was securely back in my chair, the weight of the incident settled in. My earlier premonition, the sense of foreboding I had tried to dismiss, had nearly become our grim reality. The irony of having recently willed my van to Mr. Fish, only to nearly meet our end within it, was a dark twist of fate I couldn't ignore. Yet, as we resumed our journey, a newfound sense of peace enveloped me. The belief that we had somehow averted our destined calamity allowed me to embrace the remainder of our trip with an open heart.

The thrill of four-wheeling through the rugged terrain, the laughter and camaraderie that filled the air, were all the more precious in the shadow of what could have been.

As we returned home, unscathed and enriched by the experience, I couldn't help but reflect on the mysterious forces at play. The revision of my will, the premonition, and our narrow escape were acts in a mystery too complex to fully comprehend. Yet, they underscored a profound truth—the journey of life is unpredictable, and sometimes, the most significant moments are those we narrowly miss.

31

The summer evening whispered secrets as Ariana and I ventured onto the deck, a shared sanctuary where I dared to peel back the veil on my world of enigmatic encounters. Our bond, undefined yet unmistakably profound, was poised on the cusp of a deeper revelation. Yet, as the night sky unveiled its spectacle, little did I anticipate how the aftermath would reshape the contours of our connection.

Late summer's embrace held us gently as we stepped into the openness of the deck, the air charged with the anticipation of the unknown. Our relationship, nestled in the gray zone between caregiving and something more elusive, was about to be tested against the backdrop of the cosmos.

The decision to share my experiences with the orbs and the enigmatic phenomena that had long shadowed my existence wasn't taken lightly. Yet, in Ariana's presence, I found an oasis of acceptance, a willingness to explore the uncharted without the shackles of judgment. It was this openness that emboldened me, prompting me to unveil the mysterious sounds captured near crop circles, an auditory gateway to the inexplicable.

As the otherworldly tones unfurled into the night, we sat in a companionable silence, our senses attuned to the slightest whisper from the beyond. The moment was ripe with potential, a thread of connection weaving between us as we delved into the shared act of listening, of reaching out.

Then, slicing through the serenity, a vibrant streak of green ignited the sky, a spectacle both mesmerizing and surreal. Starlink's satellites, Elon Musk's celestial train, paraded above us, their ethereal glow a spectacle that transcended the ordinary. Her reaction was a mirror to the wonder of the moment, eyes wide with astonishment, a reflection of the pure, unadulterated awe that the unexpected sight evoked.

The experience, though grounded in the technological marvels of our age, seemed to transcend its earthly origins in Ariana's eyes. It was a revelation, a glimpse into the boundless possibilities that the night sky held, a moment that, for her, was untainted by the skepticism that often-greeted tales of the mysterious. I did mention to her that what we witnessed could be explained by some people as StarLink, although after witnessing this I had my doubts that this was from our world.

Her departure that evening was buoyed by an eagerness to share, to spread the wonder of what we had witnessed. Yet, upon her return, the light of open-mindedness that had so brightly illuminated her gaze seemed dimmed. The recounting of our encounter, once a shared experience of wonder, had been subjected to the scrutinizing lens of Ariana's circle, their skepticism casting long shadows over using the crop circle noises to attract the unknown.

The shift was palpable, a transformation shaped not by her own doubts but by the weight of others' disbelief. The skepticism that now laced her words was an unfamiliar garment, ill-fitting and jarring, a barrier that rose, unbidden, between us. The deck, once a bridge to the extraordinary, had become a silent witness to the erosion of wonder, to the insidious creep of doubt.

In my eagerness to share the depths of my world, I had overlooked the fragile nature of belief, its vulnerability to the tides of skepticism that ebb and flow in the collective consciousness. The lesson was a poignant one, a reminder of the delicate dance between revealing and concealing, between the light of shared wonder and the shadows cast by disbelief.

As the summer waned, the lesson of that night lingered, a bittersweet symphony of revelation and retreat. The deck, our once-shared platform for celestial communion, stood as a testament to the transformative power of experience and the profound impact that the acceptance or rejection of the unknown can have on the human heart.

32

The evening of Halloween, draped in the playful guise of Storm and Charles Xavier, Ariana and I found ourselves ensnared in an unexpected situation. What began as an evening of sugary delights and comic book homage soon morphed into a series of eerie occurrences that left us questioning the very fabric of our reality.

The autumn chill wrapped around my home as we prepared to welcome the night's parade of ghouls and superheroes. Our costumes, a nod to the mighty X-Men, felt like more than mere attire they were a bridge to a world where the fantastic was possible, where the lines between human and superhuman blurred. I, embodying Charles Xavier, found a strange kinship with the character, his wheelchair-bound existence mirroring my own, his mind-reading prowess an echo of my yearnings for deeper connections.

Ariana, as Storm, was a vision of power and grace, her costume a testament to the character's mastery over the elements. We sat, anticipation buzzing between us, behind the shield of the front door, ready to dispense treats to the night's adventurers.

As the doorbell chimed its first summons, we sprang into action, our roles momentarily suspended as we greeted the young revelers with smiles and sweets. The light from the porch cast ghostly silhouettes through the frosted glass, a prelude to each visitation.

Yet, as the night unfurled, a curious pattern emerged. The doorbell's ring, a herald of laughter and chatter, began to betray its purpose. Four times it rang, each a phantom call with no shadowy figures to presage their approach. We opened the door to emptiness, the night air carrying no hint of mischief or flight.

The mystery deepened with each unaccompanied chime, a puzzle that seemed to laugh in the face of logic. We were ensconced in my home, the opaque windows our silent sentinels, yet they bore no witness to these invisible visitors.

Ariana's thoughts veered towards the extraterrestrial, her mind alight with the possibilities of our recent foray into the unknown, the crop circle recordings still fresh in our shared memory. Could our attempt to reach out have been answered, not with a grand appearance of UFO's or aliens, but with a playful, almost mischievous, interaction?

I wrestled with the notion, the skeptic in me clashing with the part that had seen and felt things beyond the mundane. The doorbell's unbidden calls, on the night when the veil between worlds is thinnest, seemed to dance on the edge of the inexplicable.

As the clock tolled the end of All Hallows' Eve, the mystery remained, wrapped in the shroud of the night. The unclaimed rings ceased as abruptly as they had begun, leaving us with more questions than answers. In the quiet that followed, as we packed away our superhero personas, we were left to ponder the nature of our uninvited, unseen guests.

Was it a playful spirit, a glitch in the mundane, or had our call into the vast unknown been answered with a gentle nudge, a reminder that the universe is far more whimsical and interconnected than we dare to imagine? The mystery of that Halloween night remains, a curious footnote in our journey through the extraordinary, a whisper from the cosmos that we are not alone.

33

On the early morning of November 6, 2023, I found myself teetering on the brink of an otherworldly revelation. Roused from a deep slumber yet choosing to linger in the darkness with my eyes sealed shut, I was unprepared for the journey that awaited me—a journey that would blur the lines between dream and waking reality, delivering a message of cosmic proportions.

In the stillness of the early morning, I lay motionless, hiding in the remnants of a fading dream. It was a ritual of mine, this deliberate delay in greeting the day, a momentary pause before the world rushed in. Yet, something within urged me to break the routine, to open my eyes and embrace the dawn. What met my gaze was not the familiar contours of my room but the vast, imposing expanse of Glenwood Canyon.

There, beneath the towering cliffs, I lay, staring into the abyss of the morning sky. It was there, amidst the blueish sky, that the three orbs appeared, their silent vigil a haunting echo of my past encounter. Their presence was both majestic and foreboding, a reminder of a connection forged in curiosity and wonder.

Without words, without sound, a profound understanding washed over me. It was as if the very essence of their message was woven into the fabric of my consciousness. The orbs, they communicated telepathically, held the power to reshape our world in a blink, to erase the scars of human recklessness by melting the polar ice

Interpretation of Glenwood Canyon. Created using Midjourney AI.

caps, a dire warning of the results should we continue our path of environmental destruction.

The message spoke of ancient cycles, of times when the earth itself was cleansed by flood and turmoil enacted by the orbs, a reference to the cataclysmic events of the Younger Dryas. It was a chilling reminder of the impermanence of civilizations, of the delicate balance that sustains life on this planet.

Then, as suddenly as the vision appeared, it was shattered by a sound of unimaginable intensity. It was a noise that seemed to emanate from the very core of the orbs, a sonic frequency that felt as though it could rend the very fabric of existence. The force of it jolted me back to reality, back to the safety of my bed, leaving me to question the boundaries between dream and wakefulness.

The aftermath of the encounter lingered throughout the day, a persistent ringing in my ears that dulled the world around me. It was a stark reminder of the encounter, a phantom echo of the message that had been imparted. The experience left me with a deep sense of responsibility, a renewed urgency to heed the warning and advocate for change.

That night in November was more than just a dream, it was a clarion call from beyond, a plea from the cosmos to recognize our role as stewards of this fragile indigo sphere we call home. It was a reminder that our actions have consequences far beyond our immediate perception, and that the time to act is now, lest we face the same fate as civilizations lost to the sands of time.

Interpretation of orbs melting the polar ice caps. Created using DALL-E AI.

34

The echo of the crash jarred me from my thoughts, a sound so startling and out of place it could only herald the onset of another inexplicable event in a series that had come to define my November. The peculiar incidents that commenced with the Halloween doorbell mysteries were mere harbingers of the bewildering phenomena that were to unfold.

The air in the kitchen hung heavy with a stillness that belied the chaos to come. As the sudden clamor reverberated through the house, a surge of unease gripped me. Venturing into my room, the sight that greeted me defied logic, a large, 4x4 painting, previously propped securely against the wall, now lay in ruins at the room's center, as if propelled by unseen forces. The impossibility of the scenario left me grappling with questions for which I had no answers.

Days melded into one another, each bringing its own enigma. A spray bottle, previously perched on a bathroom shelf, found its way to the middle of the floor, joined by a paint can lid that had inexplicably journeyed from the laundry room. The normalcy of my daily life was being punctured by events that seemed to whisper of an unseen presence, each occurrence more baffling than the last.

The phenomena escalated with the appearance of white pillars descending from the sky, a sight dismissed by others but which filled me with an inexplicable dread. Then, the eerie melody from

the piano in the vacant basement apartment below, a tune played in the absence of its usual occupants, sent shivers down my spine.

Then came the unmistakable sound of wood sliding across the floor, a precursor to the ceiling fan's unbidden activation. The fan, with its history of peculiar behavior, seemed to be a conduit for whatever forces were at play, its sudden illumination casting my surroundings in an eerie light.

As I confided in a caregiver about the strange occurrences, her question about auditory experiences lingered in the air. No sooner had the word "no" left my lips than a disembodied "hello" permeated the room, a chilling affirmation of the unseen presence that seemed to be making itself increasingly known.

Confronted with the relentless progression of unexplained events, I found myself at a crossroads. The allure of the unknown, which had once captivated me, now seemed a Pandora's box I had unwittingly opened. The realization that my exploration might have invited these occurrences weighed heavily on me, prompting a retreat from the pursuit of answers that lay beyond our understanding.

In the wake of these experiences, my fascination with the realms beyond our comprehension began to wane, giving way to a newfound interest in the tangible, earthly potential of robotics. Perhaps, in the mechanical and the explainable, I would find the solace that the mysteries of the universe had eluded, a grounding in the face of the inexplicable that had come to unsettle my world.

35

Suddenly awakened in the eerie stillness of a January dawn, I found myself disoriented, with no evident cause to disrupt the silence that had enveloped my sleep at precisely 4:00 AM. My heart raced, a drumbeat loud in the quiet of the early morning, as I struggled to untangle myself from the heavy duvet. The room was cold, the kind of cold that seeps into your bones, but a shiver that ran through me wasn't entirely from the chill in the air.

With a shaky body, my breaths came in short, ragged gasps. I needed to calm down. Focusing on the rise and fall of my diaphragm, I began the breathing meditation that had become my lifeline in these hauntingly early hours. Inhale. The cool air filled my lungs, a faint, musty scent of the bedroom mingling with it. Exhale. My shoulders dropped, the tension bleeding away as if it were being drawn out by the night itself.

The silence of the room wrapped around me like a cocoon as I sank deeper into relaxation, the initial panic slowly receding to the back of my mind. But it was the dreams that lingered, vivid and unsettlingly real, more like memories than mere figments of my imagination.

I remember waking up in the dream just as I had in reality, but something was off. The room bathed in an ethereal glow, the kind that you'd think was the morning light if it weren't for the clock mockingly flashing 4:00 AM. It was that light, too bright, too white, seeping through the edges of the window shade, that set my heart racing all over again.

With a dry throat, I muttered to the emptiness of my room, "They're back." The words felt curious, tasting of interest and wonder. It was a silent acknowledgment of the unreal becoming my reality, of visitors in the night that belonged more to the realm of fiction than to this world.

The next moment, a blackness enveloped me, a void where time and space lost all meaning. When I came to, the surroundings were alien, the air thick with a tension that made it hard to breathe. And there, atop me, was a being, its form unsettling in its unfamiliarity—brown, elongated, its eyes a pair of dark pools set too close on its face. It was like staring into the face of an otherworldly creature, one that defied all logic and understanding.

In an instant, the creature morphed, the air rippling around it as if reality itself was warping. The familiar face of my therapist flickered into existence, a holographic mask meant to soothe, to deceive. Its voice, when it came, was a jarring, garbled mess, a stark contrast to the perfect illusion it projected. "Your resilience, your strength, your DNA, it's... precious," it said, its message clear despite the discordant sounds.

The surreal encounter, the twisted communion, it all felt disturbingly intimate, a violation of the most personal kind. And then, just as suddenly as it had begun, it was over. I awoke, gasping for air, back in the sanctuary of my room, the morning light now a gentle caress rather than an intruder.

The encounter haunted me, trailing me like a shadow as I moved through the day. The sight of my therapist, the reality of her being pregnant and having laryngitis, it all blurred the lines between dream and waking life, leaving me to question the very fabric of my existence.

Interpretation of the creature before it morphed. Created using Midjourney AI.

It was in the following days, as the dreams persisted, that the weight of my experiences began to truly press down upon me. Each night, a repetition of the same bizarre reproduction ritual, until suddenly, as inexplicably as they had begun, they ceased.

The silence that followed was deafening, a void where once there had been a loudness of fear and confusion. I found myself adrift, caught between two worlds, neither of which I fully understood.

It wasn't until a chance encounter with a podcast, a story so eerily like my own, that the pieces began to fall into place. The words of Whitley Streiber, speaking of their breeding program with humans echoed through my mind, a mirror to my own experiences. It was a revelation, a validation, and yet, it cast a shadow of doubt over everything I thought I knew.

The realization that I might not be alone in this, that others might have shared in this unimaginable reality, was both a comfort and a curse. The fear of disbelief, of being seen as a mere imitator, loomed large, a barrier to the truth.

In the end, I chose silence, a retreat into the shadows where my story might remain my own, untainted by skepticism or accusation. It was a decision born of self-preservation, a means to protect the fragile thread of sanity I clung to.

But even in the quiet, the questions lingered, a whisper in the dark that refused to be silenced. What was real? What was mere fantasy? And in the end, did it even matter? The line between the two had blurred, leaving me in a liminal space where truth and fiction danced in the shadows of my mind.

36

As the twilight of my journey casts long shadows behind me, I find myself in the quietude of reflection, the echoes of my past painting a portrait rich with the hues of discovery, adversity, and transformation. The essence of my narrative, encapsulated in the curious incident with the cassette tape in my grandmother's house, has been the relentless pursuit of the unseen, the unexplained, and the unfathomable.

In the labyrinth of life, each twist and turn brought its own revelations, its own set of challenges that molded me not just in physique but in spirit. From the innocent mischief of a child to the profound quests of my later years, the thread of curiosity remained unbroken, a signal that guided me through the darkest nights and the brightest days.

The lessons learned were not just of the world around me but of the universe within. The psychic's predictions, once a forbidden fruit, became a metaphor for the knowledge that lay just beyond the grasp of my understanding, urging me to reach further, to question deeper. It was this insatiable curiosity that led me to explore realms both physical and metaphysical, to seek connections with the mysterious orbs and to listen for messages in the silence between stars.

My transformation, though intangible, is as real as the ground beneath my feet. The person who once stood at the threshold of grandma's den, heart racing with anticipation, has journeyed through myriad experiences, each leaving its indelible mark. The challenges faced, the obstacles overcome, have fortified my resolve, imbuing me with a resilience that time cannot erode.

As I pen these closing words, the lessons of my journey unfurl before me like a scroll, each chapter a testament to the power of the human spirit to seek, to strive, and to understand. The journey has taught me that the true essence of life lies not in the destinations reached but in the wisdom gleaned along the way.

To those who have rolled with me, in reality or through the pages of this memoir, I extend my deepest gratitude. Your companionship, whether tangible or spiritual, has been the light in my darkest hours, the warmth on the coldest nights.

Looking to the horizon, the future is an unwritten chapter, a canvas awaiting the brushstrokes of tomorrow. The pursuit of the mysterious continues, the quest for understanding unquenched. The mysteries that once whispered in the shadows now beckon with the promise of new discoveries, new connections, and new beginnings.

In the grand tapestry of existence, our lives are but threads, each color, each texture contributing to the masterpiece that is the human experience. As I move forward, the lessons of the past are my compass, guiding me toward new horizons, new adventures.

And so, with a heart filled with gratitude and eyes open to the wonders yet to unfold, I roll, into the future, embracing the unseen, undaunted by the unknown. For in the quest for understanding, in the pursuit of the unfathomable, lies the true essence of our being.

Thank you, dear reader, for being a part of my journey. May the path ahead be lit with the light of knowledge, the warmth of companionship, and the courage to embrace the unseen.

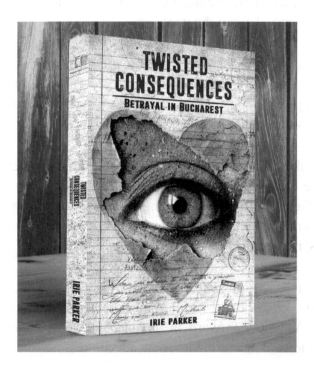

Irie Parker's "Recurring Consequences" is a unique, engrossing thriller. Tyson, a protagonist with a disability, is authentically portrayed, navigating unexpected twists and deep psychological layers. Parker skillfully builds suspense and complex character interactions, making this a must-read for fans of psychological thrillers with a fresh perspective. Definitely recommended.

- (Amazon Book Review)

Acknowledgment of AI Assistance

This memoir was created with the assistance of various AI technologies, including OpenAI's LLM, MidJourney AI, DALL-E, and Photoshop's generative AI. These tools played a significant role in drafting, organizing, and refining the content, as well as generating visual elements that complement the narrative. While these AI technologies were instrumental in the creation process, all the personal experiences, reflections, and insights shared in this memoir are entirely my own.

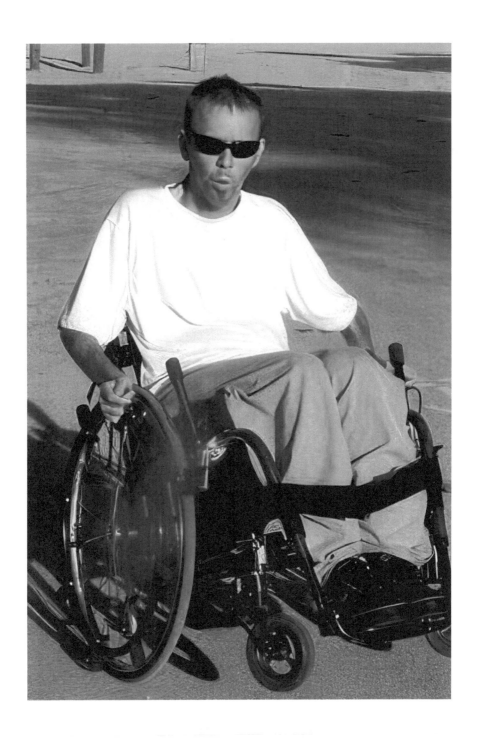

Made in United States
Troutdale, OR
08/04/2024

21751768R00070